THE PIPE

*A serious yet diverting treatise
on the history of the pipe and all its appurtenances,
as well as a factual withal philosophical discussion
of the pleasurable art of selecting
pipes, smoking, and caring for them.*

BY GEORGES HERMENT

Translated by Arthur L. Hayward
Illustrated by George Poole and Paul Jensen

SIMON AND SCHUSTER
New York

Dedicated

TO ALL

TRUE PIPE SMOKERS

Contents

CONTENTS

Part Three

Part Four

Part Five

Introduction

A<small>T THE</small> *risk of disappointing the reader on the very threshold of this book, we feel it our duty to warn him that it has been written in the manner of a poem, by a flash of happy inspiration.*

As may well be the case with a poem, twenty years of meditation and brooding have scarcely been sufficient incubation to produce these few pages. In the light of these observations it will be easier to grasp what follows:

Treated in a purely technical style, a subject such as ours could not have failed to rebuff the simple amateur. On the other hand the veteran or professional smoker would have considered it too superficial to satisfy his requirements, not full enough to fulfill his desires.

*Thanks to a complete and exhaustive knowledge of the subject, after years of experience and research, we have been able to conceive this work in its fullest scope and present it to the reader just as the spirit came to us—*currente calamo.

Such has been our aim. Have we attained it? The reader, be he veteran or amateur, must be the judge.

G. H.

THE PIPE

Part One

BROACHING THE SUBJECT

THE PIPE was known in Europe even before the introduction of tobacco. History informs us that the Celts smoked aromatic herbs in iron pipes of their own making. In the course of archæological excavations among ancient ruins in Holland, Ireland, Italy, Germany, Russia, Switzerland (notably in the Avenches, Morgues and Saint-Prex districts) iron and terra-cotta artifacts (presumably those of wood having offered less resistance to the ravages of time) have been unearthed, the shapes of which can leave no doubt as to the purposes for which they were made.* In Ireland such objects are so frequently dug up that they are known as "Danish Pipes," or in Scotland as "Fairy" or "Elfin Pipes."†

The oldest known pipes discovered up to now are the neolithic pipes found in the "mounds" of North America and dating back to its first inhabitants; that is to say—five to six thousand years

---

* In the famous fresco at Pompeii, commonly known as the "Knucklebone Players," one of the figures is smoking a pipe.

† They are usually made of earthenware; in the Cantons of Basle and the Bernese Jura, however, they are mostly of iron, and may date from the Gallo-Roman period. Many of those found in Britain and Ireland are now known to be broken stems of Elizabethan and Stuart pipes. Quantities of such pieces have been dug up when clearing the ruins of bombed areas in London.

ago. Indeed, the conception of the pipe, even in its visual and tactile forms, is lost in the dimness of past ages.

Apart from such early origins it is clear that the honor of having introduced the pipe into Europe does not belong, as is commonly thought, to the famous Jean Nicot (*c.* 1530-1600), but to the Spanish and Portuguese sailors who adopted and transformed the Indian calumet; introducing it first into the Low Countries and then into England, along with exotic herb tobacco. The utensil then took the name of "Tobacco Pipe," undoubtedly to prevent confusion with any other object known as a "pipe," as, for example, a "Pipe of Wine."

It was, therefore, toward the end of the sixteenth century that the tobacco pipe made its way casually, and in its own good time, along the highways of Europe. They began to make pipes in Holland, in England, in Germany and Flanders. Even if Louis XIII did not smoke himself, he permitted his subjects to do so, contenting himself with a pinch of rappee from an ivory snuffbox. Under Louis XIV, whose victorious campaigns bore the French soldiery into countries where pipe smoking was already the custom, the habit spread throughout France and became general among the so-called lower classes. In his paternal care for his army Le Roi Soleil ordered a regular issue of tobacco to the troops, and not content with that, desired that every soldier should have his own pipe and his own flint and steel. It was doubtless at that period that Jean-Bart caused a scandal by smoking a pipe under the noses of the courtiers in the King's antechamber itself. But it is fact that the very day of this outrageous behavior the King made the great corsair a commodore of the Royal Fleet. What did the court gentlemen think of that? History does not relate, any more than it explains that it was precisely because Jean-Bart had the self-possession to smoke his pipe that he received such high dignity; but it will be gathered from this incident that however strict Louis XIV was when it came to points of etiquette, he was troubled with few prejudices.

Up to 1830 pipe smoking appears to have been confined to the lower and middle classes. Even in this emancipated twentieth century to light a pipe in society is looked upon somewhat askance, and it should be remembered in this connection that pipes are still prohibited in casinos and certain other public places. But the pipe held its own throughout the seventeenth century, notably in the Bohemia of the artistic world. Earlier than Barthélemy (1716-95) who, in his *Art de fumer* sings the praises of pipe and cigar, the poet Prefontaine was among the first to celebrate its virtues. One of Scarron's characters in the *Roman comique* smokes a pipe. Casanova talks in his *Memoirs* of a pipe almost as fondly as he does of women. The Marquis de Sade's valet declared that his master "smoked a pipe like a pirate," and a malicious pleasantry about Crebillon *père* was that "in his lifetime he smoked more pipes than Voltaire had enemas."

The eighteenth century, sharp-witted and cynical, free-thinking and eager for novelty as it was, extended its nostrils appreciatively toward the bowl of a pipe. In Prussia Frederick William I, father of Frederick the Great, instituted a Tabakscollegium, or Tobacco College. When the members met, each kept his pipe in his mouth throughout the session, Frederick himself often occupying the chair. Not even members of the French royal family, hidebound in snobbery as they may have been, were immune to the failing; once the Dauphin surprised the princesses taking a pull at the Swiss Guards' pipes. Such goings-on could end in but one way—Revolution!

But we must wait for the Romantic period to see the vogue of the pipe in popular and general use. Such everyday expressions as "not worth a pipe of 'baccy," or "worth no more than a broken pipe" are sufficient indications of this. Before the birth of Victor

Hugo, the pipe had already got its slang name of "bouffarde" in the Grande Armée. Jean Nepoma Bouffardi was a corporal who had both arms carried away by a shell at the battle of Friedland. It is not known whether he was at the same time killed, but the next day one of his arms was found on the battlefield, the fingers still clutching his pipe. We do not know whether it was a briar or a clay; but from that day it was called a "bouffarde," and it became the mascot of his company.

In Napoleon's Grande Armée, again, we find that gallant cavalry leader Lasalle advancing to the charge with his pipe held firmly in his teeth; and it is told of him that he performed prodigies of valor in capturing a field marshal who had refused to hand over his meerschaum. "Lasalle came back to camp," Barthélemy says, "with the pipe and its owner." Oudinot received from Napoleon's hands a pipe of honor, a meerschaum in the shape of a mortar on its carriage being dragged into action. It was ornamented with diamonds and at the time was worth 30,000 francs. The Marshal's collection of pipes was, indeed, one of the most remarkable in France. Later, that of the Duc de Richelieu was very famous, and during the reign of Louis XVIII was valued at 100,000 francs. At Carlsbad the old Duke of Zweibrucken had a collection of pipes worth 100,000 florins; the King of Württemburg owned another of about the same value.

Oudinot and Lasalle were not the only Napoleonic pipe smokers. There were Kléber and Masséna, whose pipes are preserved in the Nice museum. There was Lannes, who at the battle of Essling demanded a pipe to smoke while his two legs were being amputated. Murat was a pipe smoker also, his preference being a briar representing a Triton bending backwards, his gaping mouth and throat forming the bowl. According to one of his friends, General Vandamme's house was "an arsenal of pipes."

Even Napoleon himself, on one occasion, smoked a pipe. It was, some assert, when he was in Egypt, and he smoked as a matter of diplomacy (the Mameluke Roustan having the duty of filling the bowl); others say that it was in France, at the Tuileries, where it was done only out of deference to some Persian ambassador who had made the Emperor a present of a hookah. In any event, the experiment was not repeated—nor even concluded—for His Majesty began to cough, nearly choked, and spat out the mouthpiece with a typical expression of disgust. Thereafter he was content to leave the smoking to the troops. Constant, his valet, tells us that "The Emperor was upset for at least an hour after trying to smoke; and for the future renounced a pleasure which, as he remarked, was only good for helping idlers to while away the time."

By this time we have reached the era of pipes gripped in the teeth, as developed from the long-stemmed pipe held in the hand. It was while smoking these short pipes that the young men in *Hernani* rushed into battle, as bravely as their elders had charged at Austerlitz.

In 1815, at the time of the Bourbon Restoration in France, there was a brief but noticeable reaction against the pipe. Royer Collard, a prominent statesman and philosopher, pronounced against it. It was not the thing to smoke a pipe in public (as we have observed, the inhibition holds to a certain extent to this day), and this made it obvious that an antinomy as well as an antonymy might well exist between the people and the public. But in 1830 the pipe won the battle. If the cigarette was legal currency in the street, so to speak, its competitor ended by conquering all classes, and devotees of the pipe smoked it at home. It even passed into Art in the shape of statues of famous persons sculptured, pipe in mouth. There was little likelihood of its ever really going out of fashion again.

Many museums contain remarkable collections of pipes; a French writer may, perhaps, be excused for particularizing a few in France. The museum of ceramics at Sèvres exhibits examples

1–Narghile

2–Meerschaum, billiard shape, amber stem, cased

3–French twist-opening rubber pouch

4–Oom-Paul

5–Calabash, meerschaum bowl

6–Hexagonal poker, square bit and shank

7–Plains American Indian ceremonial pipe, XVIII century

8–Shell briar churchwarden, bamboo shank

9–Billiard, military bit

10–Corncob, plastic bit

11–Dutch Baronite, porcelain with gold filigree

12–Dutch porcelain, with hand-painted landscape on bowl

13–Bulldog, saddle bit

14–Jumbo Bulldog, saddle bit

15–Slab of Macedonian briar

16–Goedewagen Dutch sailor's pipe

17–Traditional style modern churchwarden, billiard shape bowl

18–Royal Goedewagen, original style clay churchwarden

19–Windproof, wheel-flint, fluid lighter

20–Carved briar, Beethoven head

21–Apple, bent saddle bit and shank, called the "Papa"

22–Alsatian, covered porcelain bowl, with brandy well, cherrywood shank, bone bit

23–Sportsman's briar billiard, with hinged silver wind-lid

24–French cherrywood, bent stem

25–Pouch, wool plaid cover, roll-up type

1, 2, 3, 4, 5, 10, 11, 12, 16, 18, 20, 22, 24–*Courtesy of Wally Frank Ltd., New York;* 6, 13, 14, 15, 21, 25–*Courtesy of Wilke Pipe Shop, New York;* 7–*Collection of James M. Luongo;* 8, 23–*Courtesy of Alfred Dunhill Ltd., New York;* 9, 17–*Courtesy of Comoy's of London, Inc., New York;* 19–*Courtesy of Zippo.*

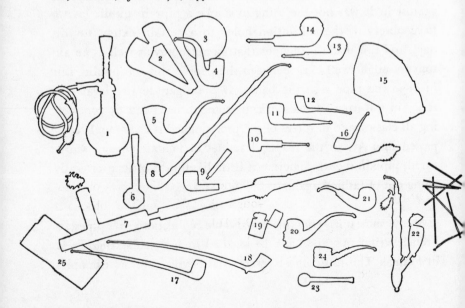

from the earliest times to the beginning of the seventeenth century. The Carnavalet Museum in Paris contains a collection of replicas and models; the Galliera, also in Paris, contains a great number of smokers' accessories, among which as well are some remarkable items that belonged to Napoleon III, Horace Vernet, George Sand, Corot and many others.

The pipe is admitted, as we have seen, almost everywhere now except in the casino (and, oddly enough, particularly in the gaming rooms of those establishments) or at diplomatic receptions and the like, notwithstanding the respectability shed on the practice by President Edouard Herriot and Prime Minister Stanley Baldwin.

It would be impossible to enumerate those of the famous who have been pipe smokers; in addition to those already mentioned we may indicate Carnot the Terrorist, Flaubert, Courbet the painter, Baudelaire, Verlaine, Rimbaud, Marshal Foch, King Albert I of Belgium. Among women, Madame de Pompadour, Vigée Lebrun, Rosa Bonheur, George Sand. Thus the pipe, the center of so much discussion and heart-burning until our own times, can now be considered one of the most common and familiar objects of everyday life.

DEFINITIONS, DIAGRAMS, EXPLANATIONS, ETC.

Dictionaries do not invariably define. Dr. Johnson says of a tobacco pipe: "A tube of clay through which the fume of tobacco is drawn into the mouth." The O.E.D.: "A narrow tube of clay, wood or other material, with a bowl at one end, for drawing in the smoke of tobacco." In French, the fact that the word "fourneau" is applied equally to a furnace and to a pipe bowl leads us into the realm of semantics; for in the well-known French *Larousse,* we find a pipe defined as an apparatus essentially formed of a furnace and a tube, used in smoking. It is impossible to rest there. *Larousse* must be consulted again as to what a furnace or bowl is, and then, what a tube.

The old dictionaries of the French Academy were more explicit, especially that of 1821: "A small earthenware tube, with a bowl at one end, for smoking tobacco." Littré says: "A tube by which smoke is inhaled from tobacco burned in a small receptacle at one end." In a treatise on smoking written in 1845: "The pipe is a tube, more or less long, of various shapes, connected with a furnace, through which one draws into the mouth tobacco smoke."

A gentleman who had never so much as set eyes on a pipe and, after reading a book on the subject conceived a sudden desire to smoke one, would, if he acted logically, seek a furnace capable of resisting the action of fire, for example one made of cast iron, and a tube (a cane, reed or the like) that could be easily inserted into the buccal orifice (always supposing that the gentleman in question—having first studied his *Larousse*—was bright enough not to insert therein the furnace). Having got thus far, and presuming that he has already been informed that tobacco is combustible, he will place some in the furnace (it being further assumed that he is aware that he can roll a cigarette or pack a pipe with tobacco bought in a packet). Having now overcome all obstacles he will have come to the actual point of smoking his pipe, which will inevitably lead to his being very sick, and to a doctor being summoned in the utmost haste. Indeed, in one way or another that is what happens to all smokers in the early days. Many of the world's great smokers have never forgotten that first pipe.

To get back to where we started: one must have first seen an object before the definition will convey anything; or, put otherwise, the definition of an object only teaches one what is known already. There is, therefore, no lack of clarity but an absence of illustration. A drawing always tells more than a phrase, and that is why we shall, in the following pages, have recourse to diagrams as often as may appear necessary or desirable.*

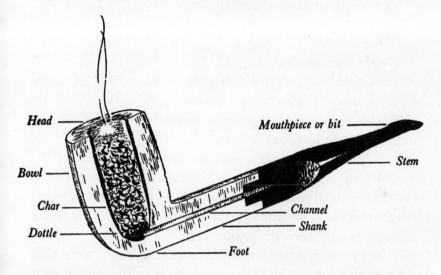

Head —   *Mouthpiece or bit* ———

Bowl —   *Stem*

Char —   *Channel*

Dottle —   *Shank*

Foot

In olden days the pipe was a measure of capacity employed in dealing with liquids. It took various forms, as shown in the following passage from Commynes' *Memoirs:* "King Edward caused his brother the Duke of Clarence to be put to death in a pipe of Malvoisie or Malmsey." For the Duke's sake we can but hope that the pipe was full and his death pangs thereby somewhat eased. "The men of the town built ramparts of great pipes for wine filled with earth," writes the chronicler Jean Molinet, in 1507.

It is possible that the tobacco pipe, the object of our researches, took its name from this measure of capacity rather than from its remote ancestors found in excavations among the ruins of the Old

* In the course of this book the reader will be obliged to make frequent reference to the above illustration. He is therefore advised to commit it to memory here and now and save himself the trouble of constantly turning back to it

and the New Worlds. As a question of semantics the word "pipe" denotes a great number of objects, animate and inanimate. It has no etymological equivalent in Latin; in very late Latin *pipa* signified a reed. Derived from or akin to this we have:

Old High German—*phifa, pfeiffe*
English—*pipe*
Danish—*pibe*
Welsh and Gaelic—*pib*.

All these would appear to be forms of the Latin, and all derive from the same root idea of *pipa,* a reed.

The sequence would, then, appear to be: reed, tube, tobacco pipe, liquid measure, cask or barrel.

This must be taken with some reservation, however, for the word is employed for a number of other objects or representations of objects. It has even been put forward that the word "pipe" comes from the noise made by the lips when drawing in smoke through the pipestem. To us, this derivation seems no more foolish than any other. Some authors, in more serious vein, assert that the word comes from the Christians of the Byzantine Empire who employed it to designate the metal tube through which the consecrated element of wine was sucked up from the chalice when the Sacrament of Communion was administered in both kinds—*pipa ad surgendum vinum calici.* Mention of such an instrument occurs in the will of the Comte de Saint-Evrard, son-in-law of Louis le Debonnair, who bequeathed a "golden pipe" to his parish church.

However this may be, the very shape of the word took on other forms in the course of the centuries. We have already seen the "bouffarde" appear in France. We shall come across the meerschaum, made of a clay once supposed to be petrified sea foam; we shall meet the simple "clay" of which, in England, two varieties prevailed; the "cutty" or short pipe, and the "churchwarden," or long one.

POINTS TO BE OBSERVED

The use of a pipe is not restricted to tobacco smoking. A pipe serves for smoking opium, hemp, and a multitude of other narcotics. Mankind has always smoked something. In antiquity it was the priests who did so. Pliny recommends coltsfoot as a sedative for a cough; he even advises inhaling it by means of a reed, in other words, a pipe. Our ancestors smoked marjoram. In explorers' narratives one constantly comes across the custom; for example, the Caribs wrap tobacco in very thin bark and, by a movement of the tongue make the smoke pass from the mouth through the nostrils, as is the habit of many cigarette smokers to this day. In India and the Pacific Islands the natives smoke cheroots, which are rolled tobacco leaves, otherwise cigars. In Siberia they smoke a sort of fungus; in Peru and Bolivia it is coca; in Turkey, India and China, opium mingled with various perfumes; in Africa, hashish and a species of hemp known as cannabis. Elsewhere it will be tea, lavender, dried fungus, aniseed, hops, sunflower seeds. More refined than others, the Hindus mix all sorts of things with their tobacco—sugar, nutmeg, and even ground bananas moistened with rose water.

From objects found in excavations in the countries already mentioned, with considerable resemblance in appearance to tobacco pipes, archæologists have come to the conclusion that tobacco must have been introduced into Europe as a narcotic superior in virtue to hemp and the other intoxicating plants of which the Scythians, in particular, made use in their orgies—not smoking them, as the Celts did, but throwing them into the fire and sniffing up the fumes.

Indeed, it would appear that the pipes we have already mentioned were used to smoke something different from tobacco, and archæologists of the greatest repute assert that it was hemp that primitive man smoked, though they give no indication of whether it was unadulterated or how it was prepared. This last hypothesis is all the more acceptable since hemp is still smoked in India which, it may be observed, has long had a record of refinement, or anyhow experience, in such matters. In this connection it should be noted that ancient pipes have also been unearthed in India.

Any disputation on the subject would be futile and lead nowhere, for in every country in the world primitive man has smoked —and mankind still smokes—a variety of plants, narcotic as well as aromatic. The Indians of the Amazon smoke yague; those of North America smoke willow bark mixed with various mysterious substances. In 1640 the explorer Jean Delaet tells of the Carib natives who lived in huts filled with smoke from pipes "with which they suck in the fumes of tobacco." After all, did we not every one of us, when young, smoke brown-paper cigars or onionskin cigarettes? In Corsica, even in the last century, a sort of nightshade related to the petunia was the national tobacco of the inhabitants.

An even closer study of the matter would, in any case, merely lead us to the conclusion not only that the pipe made its appearance on this planet before tobacco, but that the use of it had spread far and wide long before the discovery of that plant. Originally, no doubt, it was the custom to pack tobacco into a receptacle rather than roll it in the leaf. Facts exist to prove this: The Indians had invented the pipe long before they knew of such a thing as paper; the method of using tobacco rolled in paper does not go back, at least in Britain or France, much further than the 1830s, though in certain other countries, such as Spain, it is older.

The sequence is, therefore: plants, pipes, tobacco, paper.

Thus, though it is permissible to assign an origin to the words "pipe" and "tobacco," we are obliged to state that the beginnings of the custom of smoking are lost in the darkness of antiquity— which is all for the best and a great relief so far as we are concerned.

MATERIALS

There are in existence a great number of materials suitable for the making of pipes, and there are yet more to be discovered and tried out by experiment; but as these do not properly fall within the scope of this book, which for clarity's sake should really have been called *The Briar Pipe,* we shall content ourselves with describing in some detail the pipes we know personally and show, if there is room to do so, their virtues.

But to begin with, we must warn the reader against the common error—so obstinately held as to class it in the category of popular prejudices—that consists in thinking that any hard material or that any kind of wood is suitable for making a good pipe. Experience goes to prove the contrary, for wood such as chestnut, acacia, or willow, hard materials such as iron or stone, are not to be considered; whereas such soft materials as corncobs, rosewood and pumpkins offer many advantages. The hardness of the substance has, therefore, no relation to the sweet smoking of the pipe. If the Celts smoked iron pipes it was evidently because they knew nothing of the odoriferous virtues of tobacco. Hardness is only a practical advantage, and in our study of the briar root we shall see this point exemplified.

THE CLAY, PORCELAIN AND MEERSCHAUM PIPES

Up to the beginning of this century the clay pipe was, in some form or another, in very common use. It is still fairly popular. English clay pipes are first mentioned by Paul Hentzler in 1598, when he visited the Southwark Bear Garden one autumn afternoon: "At these spectacles and everywhere else the English are constantly smoking tobacco and in this manner: They have pipes on purpose made of clay, into the further end of which they put the herb, so dry that it may be rubbed into powder, and putting fire to it they draw the smoke into their mouths, which they puff out again through their nostrils, like funnels, along with it plenty of phlegm and defluxion from the head." In 1615 William Camden, of *Britannia* fame, said, "Some men from wantonness, some for health's sake, with an insatiable desire and greediness suck in the stinking smoke through an earthen pipe, which presently they blow out again through their nostrils, insomuch that tobacco shops are now as ordinary as taverns and taphouses."

These old pipes, many fine collections of which are still in existence, had the bowls leaning forward, and were some five or six inches in length; it was not until the eighteenth century that the makers began to set the bowls at right angles to the stem. There were pipemakers all over the country, each branding the pipes he made with his own trademark stamped into the wet clay. In the eighteenth century the long churchwardens were introduced, or invited.

In France the manufacture of clay pipes began in the northern districts at Givet. There as in England, the material employed was a white, plastic clay, carefully selected, kneaded, shaped but not washed, and placed in the oven. Suitable clay is found in many parts of most countries.

THE TURKISH CHIBOUK—the latter a Turkish word meaning a wand or stick, and thence a tube—consists of a bowl of red clay (rarely of metal) with a tube or stem (chibouk) made of jasmine or cherrywood, maybe some two or three feet in length. The bowl is usually rather bell-shaped, or open; the stem is terminated in an amber, bone, or tortoise-shell mouthpiece—the *imaneh*. The

Chibouk

decoration of the chibouk gives free rein to the craftsman, as you can see, but contrary to what one might expect, it has more than a purely artistic purpose, for the gaily colored cords are so tied that in the event of the various sections of the pipe coming apart, these separate pieces will not fall and be broken.

The mouth of the bowl is not always funnel-shaped; sometimes it is closed with a lid of iron or other metal. At the base of the bowl there may be several openings—sometimes as many as eight —in which additional stems can be inserted. The chibouk may therefore be considered the collective or sociable pipe *par excellence*. It changes its name from one country to another, but the use is the same; as the calumet or pipe of peace it is in some degree symbolic.

The chibouk, as such, is smoked very little in Europe, but the essentially rational principle of its form and usage has been widely adopted elsewhere for a long time.

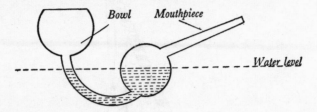

THE NARGHILE belongs to the same family as the chibouk. The bowl is of terracotta. This pipe is held in high esteem among the

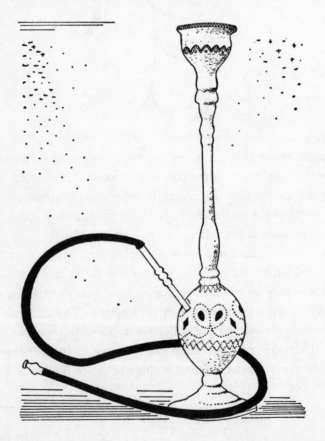

Turks and certain other peoples of Asia. To an even greater extent than its predecessor its construction (see page 16) offers antiseptic guarantees of the first order; it is, indeed, the pipe doctors dream of when prescribing for victims of nicotinism. Some authors credit the Persians with having invented the system of the narghile; others of equal weight attribute it to the Dutch; yet others to the English.

The principle of this pipe is somewhat complicated, as can be seen by our two illustrations. The bowl, cunningly housed in a beautifully made glass holder; a supple and very long tube or stem encased in gaily colored silk; a receptacle for scented water through which the smoke has to pass before reaching the mouth —all these are details that reveal a degree of civilization that, however different it may be from our own, is in no sense less enlightened. The narghile is a work of art in itself. Like the chibouk, it forms an integral part of the Oriental interior. It would, however, be incorrect to say that these handsome utensils are restricted to the service of families smoking the harmless tobacco weed; they are used for opium and other narcotics too varied to enumerate.

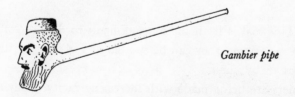

Gambier pipe

THE GAMBIER.   This was once one of the best-known shapes of clay pipe. It is named after the inventor and first maker. There are two forms of it, as illustrated above, and page 18 at *a,* and in one or other of these forms it was much favored toward the end of the nineteenth century. Verlaine smoked a gambier shaped with a cock's head; in one of Rimbaud's poems he defies the world *"une gambier aux dents";* Mallarmé smoked practically nothing else.

Painters and poets have rivaled one another in seasoning their clays. Belonging to the gambier family are the little pipes, often known as William Tells, with which the French troops on maneuvers amuse themselves by setting them up outside their tents as targets for rifle practice; but like the English Aunt Sally clays, they are of inferior quality and poor imitations of crude articles. In the choice of a clay pipe such as these, caution if not actual distrust should be the order of the day.

The genuine clay pipe is usually white, though occasional specimens are found in red clay, brown, gray, black, dull blue and

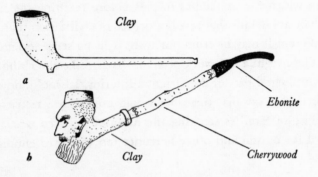

Clay

a

Ebonite

b   *Clay*   *Cherrywood*

mauve. This makes it all the more difficult to discern imitations; but with experience they can be spotted at a glance, by the touch of the lips, or by smell.

Gambiers are being made with increasing rarity. They are very brittle and, in a word, uncarriable. They have largely been replaced by the Jacob (see above) which is a less breakable pipe, with a cherrywood stem. But here, also, imitations abound, and considerable circumspection in choice is necessary.

Apart from the Jacob with its wooden stem, the disadvantage of clay pipes lies in the weakness of the stem, which is much more fragile than the bowl, for the latter can be reinforced at its mouth by a metal ring—iron, copper or any metal that does not fuse readily and is at the same time light in weight. Some makers have got over the difficulty of brittleness by producing pipes in which the lower opening houses a metal ring—or is set in one—holding

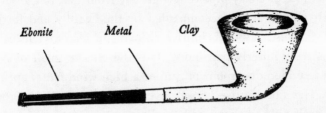

a short ebonite mouthpiece, as we see here. Unfortunately these pipes lose in taste what they gain in strength, for, as we shall see, the stem itself, when the tobacco is burning, has a great deal to do with the smell and taste of the pipe.

In France the gambier has been so popular, and still enjoys such high esteem among collectors, that it might almost be considered the national pipe, thus contrasting in every detail with the porcelain pipes of the Germans.* In England, the plain clay, whether the short "cutty" or the long churchwarden, retained its hold on the so-called lower classes, especially in the agricultural districts, until the 1914 war.

A clay pipe draws slowly. Contrary to what happens in a wooden pipe the blackish deposit left by tobacco when burned takes longer to form in clay, which appears to be less permeable than wood. The novice at smoking who has tried only a briar pipe stands a good chance of being "bowled over" by his first smoke with a clay; like as not he will throw away the pipe—with whatever else there is in him—and give up pipe smoking in disgust. Our advice is to keep a clay handy and smoke it from time to time, turn and turn about with a briar, but at ever-decreasing in-

* An officially appointed committee of eight members has been set up in France to supervise and control the manufacture of pipes. Its functions are as yet indefinite.

tervals as it begins to get seasoned. This is the only way to acquire true enjoyment of a clay, and to learn to appreciate the excellence of the material of which it is made.

The taste of a clay pipe differs greatly from that of a briar; it is slightly rough, and is accompanied by the healthy and fortifying smell of moist clay—a primitive enjoyment, secret, yielding itself with a truly miserly parsimony. It is the elusive smell of Nature when a sudden downpour of rain or a high wind has swept things clean. Has not Nature herself, even in winter, a charm that reveals itself only to those ready and eager to perceive it? It is easy to understand why so many smokers, having tried and persevered in smoking a clay pipe, never go back to a briar.

After smoking a clay pipe the portion of unused tobacco at the bottom of the bowl, called the dottle, should be of the most minute proportions. Clay seems to absorb the moisture of the tobacco more readily than does wood, and by the time the burning has reached the lower part of the bowl, the tobacco is dry and burns more completely. At first this may appear a contradiction to what we have already observed concerning the greater permeability of wood, but the fact is that the woody fiber lends itself more easily to the penetration of moisture, and consequently swells under hydro-caloric action, whereas clay and certain other hard materials remain unaffected.

THE PORCELAIN PIPE. Coming under the category of clay pipes, the porcelain pipe exhibits qualities so particular as to place it in a class of its own—notably on account of its splitting or cracking on first being smoked, especially if it has been packed to the brim of the bowl with tobacco that is too moist, or has been rammed too tightly.

Porcelain requires the utmost care from the outset if it is to be seasoned properly. It must not be treated like a wooden pipe; but if, from the start, one is successful in seasoning it to a rich color, it will be found that by this very fact it has become much less fragile and less liable to overheating. Overheating causes cracks to appear in the material and through these the nicotine oozes to the despair and disgust of the smoker.

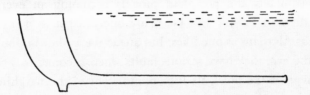

It is, of course, well known that porcelain possesses the quality —in the present instance most inconvenient—of being an excellent conductor of heat, so that the outer, enameled surface of the pipe is the same temperature as the inner surface against which the tobacco is burning. This extreme heat, it should be noted, almost always breaks the enameled surface into a network of tiny cracks. Moreover, sooner or later the novice is sure to burn his fingers. For this reason some pipes have, at the base of the bowl, a knob or protuberance as a sort of insulator, which we illustrate on this page, and by which the smoker can grasp his pipe without burning himself. This knob or protuberance is not found exclusively in porcelain pipes but on all clays or pipes made of some material that conducts heat too readily. The beard on Jacobs, for instance, is nothing but a protuberance of this nature and for this purpose.

The shiny enamel with which the porcelain pipe is coated is not an integral part, it has no connection with the material and only serves to embellish the appearance of the pipe. Porcelain is a ceramic product of a very fine paste that is nothing but kaolin or china clay, the crude material of which is a decomposition of feldspar.

A porcelain pipe is something like a gambier in its smoking. The general trend of its aroma becomes even opulent in a pipe that has mellowed thoroughly. We remember having a pipe of this sort, in the shape of a horseshoe that possessed a certain savor that makes it still a matter of keen regret that it was broken through carelessness, especially as it was beginning to season beautifully.

Unfortunately the porcelain pipe is becoming an ever rarer commodity. In France and Germany one can get as many pipes known as Alsatians as one likes; but attractive as they undoubtedly are to the eye, they have serious faults when it comes to smoking. The shape of the bowl, its lid—reminiscent of the narghile—the

Alsatian pipe

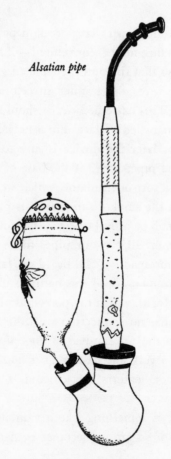

composition, shape and arrangement of the stem; all these are of a most rational design. Too rational, indeed, for the system of de-nicotinizing is not only logical but actually overlogical. Far from being as simple in principle as the narghile or the chibouk, the Alsatian has reached such a state of perfection as to be negative; the nicotine collects in quantity and exhales a fetid smell that neutralizes the natural fragrance of the smoke. This is because the method of construction is such as to hinder the normal absorption of the tobacco's moisture, which is, instead, collected in a sort of chamberpot which eventually has to be emptied of its unpleasant contents.

This very ornamental pipe—one might almost call it spectacular, for some specimens are veritable monuments, though God only knows to whom—is occasionally made of wood, deer's hoof, etc. It is greatly esteemed among certain North European nations. It is usually of huge dimensions and holds a prodigious quantity of tobacco, sometimes as much as two ounces, so it may well be called—as some do call it—their kitchen. Needless to say, there are many types, each with some special point of its own. Sufficient to add that a porcelain pipe should be in the battery of every true pipe smoker.

THE MEERSCHAUM.   There is no English name for this ma-terial; *meerschaum* is the German for "sea surf" and the same idea is preserved in the French *écume de mer,* for it was originally thought to be petrified foam. It comes from a soil sediment of the secondary and tertiary periods, being actually nothing but a white, compact, hydrous silicate of magnesia ($H_4Mg_2SI_3O_{10}$) very light in weight, hard to fuse, and occurring in strata, principally in Asia Minor. Meerschaums were greatly in vogue in the middle and early nineteenth century, but they are little met with now, owing to the rarity of the material and its costliness.

The utmost care is demanded in the manufacture of these pipes.

To begin with, the crude magnesite is boiled in milk; it is then
kneaded with wax and linseed oil. In its natural state meerschaum
does not possess the gloss for which it is so well known; before
treatment the material is of a dirty white color, blotched, and far
from attractive in appearance. It is not until the substance has acquired its lily-white hue that, cut in blocks, the bowl is roughly
shaped. Here is the sequence in the process of making a meerschaum:

1. Moistening the lump of clay.
2. Sawing into blocks.
3. Cutting and turning.
4. Rubbing and rough polishing.
5. Treating with wax and spermaceti.
6. Polishing with pumice powder or mutton bone.
7. Glazing with lime and tallow.
8. Finishing.

One of the most important operations is No. 5. The coating of
wax neutralizes the volatile products of combustion; a pipe made
simply of meerschaum would just carbonize and soon become un-
smokable.

Meerschaum can be divided into two categories:

1. Pipes cut directly from the block. These are the finest in
appearance and the scarcest, coming from beds of the material at Eski-Chehar, in Anatolia. The rejects of Class 1 pipes
can be used for making the pipes enumerated in Class 2.

2. Pipes of inferior quality made from artificial magnesite,
casein, burnt magnesia, oxide of zinc and waste matter. Such
pipes are labeled as of Austrian meerschaum—being made,
indeed, in that country. With these may be classed the clay
meerschaum, which is a variety of carbonated lime, also
found in beds; another type known in France as De Gou-

dron or Tar, is made from calcined red magnesite, and is usually coated with black, blackish or purple varnish.

In this second category may be included a great number of pipes made from artificial meerschaum. This is concocted of a mixture of siliceous and magnesia substances, sometimes a white of egg reduced to a paste. The inferior nature of these pipes reveals itself by a lack of porousness and lightness, but more markedly by their highly dubious appearance. Casein, burned magnesia, oxide of zinc and other substitute substances are likely to deceive only those smokers who, not having eyes to perceive the fraud, lack also the sense of taste to savor it.

It should be noted that pipes manufactured at Nîmes are likewise made from magnesite found in the neighborhood of that city. It may be suggested, moreover, that *écume de mer* may even be derived from Culm, the town near which the substance is found. Be that as it may, the material in question is sometimes called white soapstone or talc, but it differs from true talc in texture, being stronger and more absorbent. It must not be confused with Constantinople orosite, from which ordinary pipes are made in Turkey; this substance is also found in tertiary rocks in the vicinity of Paris.

Meerschaum is a substance of considerable luxury from which the most artistic pipes are made. The seat of the industry is at Paris. The first French maker was a certain Cardon, at one time well known as the author of a book entitled *Musée des fumeurs*, the *Smoker's Treasury*, which appeared in 1866. Many accomplished French smokers admit of nothing but the meerschaum. E. Clerc, for instance, divides all pipes into two categories; in the first he lists metal, porcelain and even wood as "nonabsorbent" and consequently inferior. In the second he places pipes made of any sort of clay, as being capable of being impregnated. Those in the first category are, according to him, merely contrivances to burn tobacco. "A pipe," he says eloquently, "is the very reverse to a fireplace. We find ourselves in the presence of an alembic in which the operation known as dry distillation is performed. Wherever dry distillation takes place a product is formed known as pyridin; this liberates the camphor of tobacco, or nicotine, an odorous, bland product without the presence of which we should none of us be smokers. The meerschaum and the clay pipe are those that best liberate this substance, hold it, collect it, and with each smoke permit its savor to be increasingly appreciated."

The physical qualities of meerschaum are imperceptible, both on account of their lack of any appreciable weight, and from the elusiveness of their taste. The touch of it is very agreeable to the lips. Its chief recommendation to the barbarian who tries a meerschaum pipe for the first time—knowing nothing about it—is the readiness with which it seasons even after the fourth or fifth smoke. The effluvium is heady, nourishing without being heavy. The pipe should be seasoned with care, respect and regularity so as not to spoil the fragile nature of the material or damage the grain; the interior and exterior surfaces alike of the bowl should be subjected to the effects of patient and tender smoking. *The Art of Seasoning a Pipe (L'art de culotter une pipe)* in Courteline's remarkable anthology only strikes home to those who have never seasoned a meerschaum. It makes others smile, though for different reasons—on the one hand because of the author's talent, on the other in amusement at his mistakes; all of which goes to show that when one encroaches upon specialized territory it is rare to escape without making a capital blunder.

Meerschaum is a substance of extreme sensibility; the novice must appreciate this before anything else. If, for example, having smoked a pipe he were to lay it immediately upon a marble-topped table, in all probability it would split, as indeed would many other pipe materials, though more rarely briar. As a matter of technology it may be observed that wood does not split, it cracks. In cabinet-making, sylviculture and other work connected with wood and trees, a crack is a fissure caused by desiccation.

To hold a meerschaum properly is a good step forward toward an understanding of its nature.

E. Clerc, the laureate of the meerschaum whom we have already quoted, pursues his lyrical discourse in praise of the pipe in words too good to be quoted other than verbatim: "The meerschaum is the queen of pipes. It is impracticable for the smoker of today since it is fragile and terribly costly; but when all this is admitted and granted, it remains the queen and no shadow can in any way be cast upon its merits. These merits are both exterior and interior. Exteriorly, of all pipes the meerschaum alone has the faculty of mellowing into a truly marvelous range of colors. These hues progress from a golden white to a rich brown, passing through the delicate pink of a china rose, a faint yellow, a golden yellow, pale orange, pinky brown, a light leather brown, warm brown, red brown, dark brown to an eventual black."

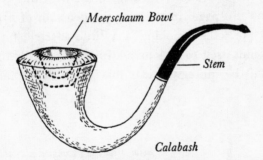

Meerschaum Bowl

Stem

Calabash

A whole chapter might well prove insufficient to exhaust the subject of the meerschaum and certain other pipes that derive from it, such as the calabash, some of these latter having a savor of their own that comes, as it were, between the clay and the briar.

In conclusion, the best advice we can give the novice is to start on a briar, and slowly accustom himself to a clay; in time he may even become worthy to smoke a meerschaum.

WOOD PIPES

Apart from those made from the root of the briar there are two principal types of wood pipes to be considered.

THE ROSEWOOD PIPE is made of the delicately scented wood of the Brazilian rosetree, known in French as *palissandre*. It is of medium hardness and in color ranges from a purplish brown to burnt sienna. It comes mostly from the West Indies. These pipes are becoming increasingly scarce as they are no longer made; this is a great pity as the wood has a very special quality of its own and imparts a delicate taste that can be obtained in no other way. The only defect in these pipes is that they were made without an ebonite mouthpiece, which meant that the grip of the teeth and the action of the saliva not only spoiled the stem in time but made it unhygienic. The fortunate owners of rosewood pipes are advised, therefore, to have them fitted with the little gadget illustrated on this page. In this way the demands of hygiene will be met and the actual smoking very little affected, for the rosewood pipe lends itself to such an addition more easily than would a clay. It will be quite sufficient that the little ebonite mouth-

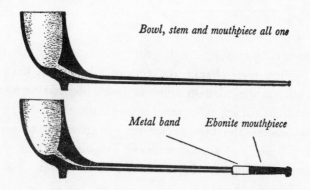

Bowl, stem and mouthpiece all one

Metal band   *Ebonite mouthpiece*

piece and its metal adapter should be placed as far as possible from the bowl and be as small as possible.

In the writer's personal experience the rosewood pipe exercised a hypnotic—or at any rate soporific—effect on the smoker. Although the taste is somewhat rough, even harsh, the smoke is insidious in its charm, especially in the first pipeful and, of course, according to the time and manner of smoking; it tends to a sense of well-being, even when the pipe is smoked out of doors. Pipes made of this particular wood are usually small, with little thickness in the walls of the bowl, thus tending to become hot; so they sometimes are made with the small butt shown in the clay pipe illustrated on page 18.

THE CHERRYWOOD is made from the wood of the wild cherry which is, like rosewood, a substance which furnishes the material for very pleasant-smoking pipes. These pipes are made in the simplest manner; the piece of wood, when it has been seasoned artificially or otherwise, is cut into blocks from which the bowls are turned and hollowed out. To the bowl a stem is added, made from a slender branch of the same tree and fitted with an ebonite mouthpiece (see below). This is the form these pipes usually take, but the best examples—and consequently the most costly—

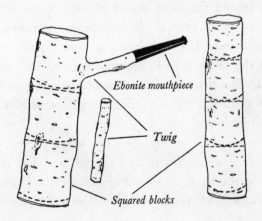

Ebonite mouthpiece

Twig

Squared blocks

have bowl and stem all of a piece, as is also illustrated. The advantage of this is obvious.

The taste of this cherrywood pipe is rather strong, somewhat heavy, slightly aromatic—a taste that many veteran smokers cannot tolerate but for which others have a real liking. The effect is as though the wood had never been properly seasoned; in this lies the secret charm of this shrub. It is worth noting in this connection that even when not alight the cherrywood keeps its delicious smell better than any other pipe, the meerschaum not excepted.

Cherrywood has the defect of becoming very soon charred. The wood burns faster than it expands; it seems passive rather than active. The seasoning is essentially internal. When selecting a pipe it is advisable to choose one on the large side. There are plenty of these—some even so big that they serve as advertisements for pipemakers or tobacconists. Far from their size being a disadvantage it may be said that the bigger and heavier the pipe, the better it smokes.

Cherrywood pipes are always made with the bark intact; it is, indeed, an integral part. It is not left on for local color or for a mere whim; there is good reason for it, as much from the point of view of combustion as of strength. The pipe could hardly be made more salable by polishing or varnishing; whereas if the bark were removed the bowl would be more liable than in any other wood to crack or split at the earliest opportunity. This often happens, indeed, even when the bark is left on, for the resistance of this latter is in an opposite sense to that of the grain of the wood. The first pipes to be smoked must not be packed too tightly nor to the brim; nor should they be smoked too quickly, especially out of doors.

Mention must here be made of the wood of the cultivated cherry tree. It is more brittle, less supple, and less resistant to heat, as also is the bark. As in the case of beasts, it may be said that domestication has robbed the wood of three quarters of its primitive qualities; all the same, a couple of medium-sized pipes of this wood may well be kept in the smoker's battery.

OTHER MATERIALS

Halfway between the wood pipe and the clay may be said to come the Moorish pipe, the commonest form of which is a mutton bone—the tibia—opened at both ends. The larger end is hollowed out as a bowl, the smaller forms the mouthpiece (see below). This pipe is known as the "adham," which is the Arabic word for a bone. As a general rule the more sophisticated Moors use a very similarly shaped pipe with a wooden bowl and a copper tube as stem called a "touba," also illustrated below. What may be styled

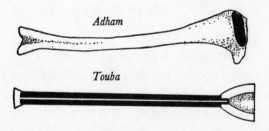

Adham

Touba

the bowl holds very little tobacco—five or six whiffs at most. When the pipe is out it is enough to use a straw or piece of wire to push through the bone and push out the ash.

Although not made from bone, in this category should be included the pipe used by certain small tribes of Central Africa, an affair so bulky and heavy that the smoker, like a saxophone player, needs a cord round his neck to support it.

To exhaust the subject of the various local forms and shapes of pipes would need a treatise in itself. A great number of other materials are employed such as the maize or corncob, a great favorite in the southern states of the U.S.A., whence it originates; the asbestos pipe, made in what are termed Dublin shapes and generally varnished black—this pipe is remarkable for its peculiar taste, which is of a slightly burnt flavor. There is the calabash, made from a kind of gourd; others of ebony or some rare wood, of metal, or even stone. The ardent smoker with some knowledge of wood can make a pipe for himself from any piece that seems suitable and adapted to the purpose. Nor must we forget the calumet, or pipe of peace (from Latin *calamus,* a reed) which is usually made of wood and provided with a rosewood stem and mouthpiece ornamented with copper and rare stones. Whatever the material of which it is made, and no matter by what name it is known, it is none the less the ancestor of the pipe, even if not the pipe of peace.

THE BRIAR ROOT

Among all the materials from which pipes are made we have reserved a special section for this, the substance best known and the basis, indeed, of this book. It is the root of the briar to which we allude, the material of the briar pipe.

And here, before any other explanation is made, it is essential to state that the briar, from which the pipe is made, is not the briar or wild rose of the hedgerows. In our connotation the word is a corruption of the French *bruyère,* or heath tree, and it is sometimes spelled "brier." The name has stuck as the manufacture of good briars is practically confined to France, where the heath root was first used and is still largely grown. Throughout this book any and every reference to the briar is to the heath root. It should also be explained that there are two varieties of this root, known in France as *bruyère blanche* and *bruyère mauve,* white or purple heather. Of these only the white is of interest to us; the purple heath roots are useless for pipes.

The briar (from Low Latin *brugaria*, itself derived from Celtic *brug*, a bush) is a low shrub found throughout Europe. The material from which pipes are made is almost exclusively obtained from the wide-spreading roots of the variety *Erica arborea*, which flourishes especially in France and other Mediterranean countries. In Corsica and parts of Italy the bulky stem of this shrub is sometimes employed.

We would take this opportunity of warning the reader against an abuse perpetrated by certain less reputable makers who, when once their makes are established on the market, do not hesitate to foist on the public inferior pipes, just as carefully varnished but cut to a large extent from what smokers incorrectly call "the branch." This "branch" is nothing but the least even-grained, least well-bound and worst in every way of the briar roots; but the use of it means a profit of 80 per cent to 90 per cent to the maker. The customer with his eyes open will not be deceived by such pipes. However reputable the trademark the astute smoker will never allow himself to forget that good advertising does not necessarily make a good article, and that, whatever its trademark or brand, a "branch" is far removed indeed from the genuine root of the briar.

Selection is made of a very dry, hard root, maybe of a hundred years' growth. This is examined by a craftsman who extracts from it any pebbles or other extraneous matter that may have got embedded. It is then sawn into cubes, which are cut roughly into the desired shapes—curved or straight, big or small. These are then turned in a lathe, sandpapered and hollowed out, before a perfect specimen can be selected. But before any of these processes the wood is kept in a bath of steam for some twelve hours; this expels the red sap and prevents splitting or cracking at later

stages of the manufacture. On an average only one perfect specimen out of fifty is obtained. The less good examples are made
into pipes of inferior quality—though this does not imply that
the wood itself is in any way inferior; it means that the grain is
not uniformly close. When choosing a pipe the best thing is to
look through the perfect specimens and select whichever appeals
most to the eye, for the chances are that it will be equally pleasing
to the taste.

The best briar roots come from the eastern Pyrenees. A certain
number of pipes are made in Paris, London and elsewhere, but it
is at Saint-Claude, in the Jura, that the manufacture has attained
its greatest excellence. This notwithstanding, what might be
termed the ethnological capital of the briar pipe is Cogolin, the
Département of the Var. The two factories at Cogolin turn out
almost all the pipes made from the Mediterranean briar. During
the war the briar roots, like many other commodities, were put
on quota. Saint-Claude exchanged ebonite—which Cogolin lacked
for making the mouthpieces—for roughly cut pipes or sawn cubes
of briar. One might sum up by saying that Saint-Claude produces
the most carefully fashioned, best-finished and most luxurious
pipes in the world, whereas Cogolin turns out the greatest number
of average good pipes. It may also be noted in passing that briar
root is used in the manufacture of a number of other objects such
as ash trays, dice, etc.

Having thus dealt with the preliminaries and generalities, let
us now turn our attention to the practical side of this book—the
study of the briar pipe.

Part Two

CHOICE OF A BRIAR

THE SHAPE. As a pipe carved from a block of wood the briar is to be found in a number of different shapes, much as pipes in any other material. According to the tastes of the smoker and fancy of the craftsmen, its outlines have varied and will continue to vary with the course of the years. It has changed with the times, but the essential shape has remained practically unchanged so far as can be ascertained by comparison with old specimens. For the shape is not a' thing that can be tampered with; it serves one end and one end only. This being so, certain shapes of briar pipes have been definitely adopted for general use. We can, once and for all, specify these accepted forms of pipes; they are illustrated on the following pages.

There is no hard and fast rule about the exact shaping of these types, nor are they of invariable measurement. The straight sides of the ordinary billiard can be higher or lower, as taste dictates; others can be more or less squat, wider or narrower at the bowl, longer or shorter in the stem. There is no question of recommending any one shape above any other; the taste and virtue of a pipe lies in the quality of the material from which it is made. Extremes of any kind, however, should be avoided. If the pipe is too squat the shape is bad, though it may be easier to slip in the pocket; the only

IDENTIFICATIONS OF THE PIPES

1–Billiard, straight-grain
2–Dublin, saddle bit
3–Bulldog, saddle bit
4–Poker, shell briar
5–Apple
6–Pear, birdseye grain
7–Churchwarden

8–Oom-Paul
9–Woodstock, shell briar, semi-bent bit
10–Prince
11–Bent Billiard
12–Pot
13–Canadian

1, 2, 3, 5, 6, 12–*Courtesy of Wilke Pipe Shop, New York;* 4–*Courtesy of Jobey;* 7, 9–*Courtesy of Comoy's of London, Inc., New York;* 8–*Courtesy of Wally Frank Ltd., New York;* 10, 11, 13–*Courtesy of Alfred Dunhill Ltd., New York.*

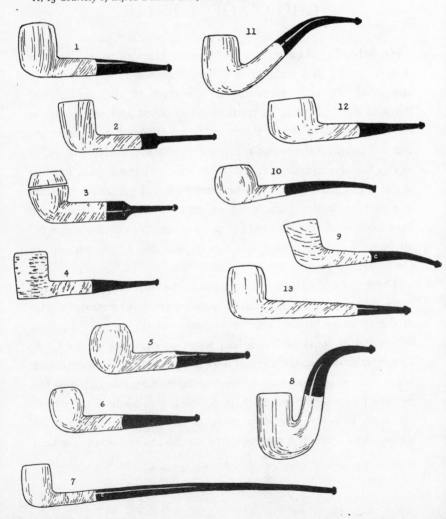

criterion is how well or badly the pipe smokes. As a rule, it may be observed, pipes carved to represent an animal or the head of some celebrity—rarely found in England—are little likely to err in this way; but too squat a pipe can easily produce the phenomenon mentioned in regard to the Turkish pipe—the tobacco will tend to burn only in the center. Of course, if that is the sort of thing the smoker likes—well and good, it is the pipe for him.

What is required above all is that the depth of the bowl should not be reduced too much, to further some whim or fancy in the design. This is made very clear by a glance at the drawing below where we see the correct method of packing, or loading a

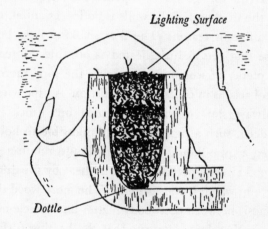

Lighting Surface

Dottle

pipe, with the suitable proportion between the bowl and the tobacco. We shall be considering elsewhere in greater detail the caliber of the bowl; whatever form the outside of the bowl may take, the interior must be of the straight-walled kind to ensure even burning. It must be admitted that all bowls do not conform to this rule, but the essential is that the top of the interior should not be narrower than the bottom, that it should resemble a V rather than a Λ. Our next illustration shows how this must apply, whatever the

outward appearance of the pipe may be. Reader and smoker alike
will understand why this should be so.

THE BOWL. *Depth and Thickness*. The really important
points about the bowl of a pipe are its depth and the thickness of
its walls. As we will go on to explain, the depth is an essential
point; but the thickness of the walls is no less essential, though for
somewhat different reasons. The best smoking is to be obtained
from a pipe that gets as little heated as possible. Moreover, there
should be plenty of wood, as this makes the pipe more generous
while the tobacco is in course of combustion. A pipe with too little
wood is always slow to yield its aroma but quick to become
heated; indeed, such a pipe is almost impossible to hold. Even if
very charred a pipe should be rich; it should retain a good basis
of clean wood already prepared to stand heat by the differences of
temperature in which it was seasoned. The more wood there is the
greater osmosis between the woody matter and the elements of the
tobacco. It is, therefore, requisite that the heating surface should
be large so that the heat thus freed can be dispersed and only to a
minimum extent reach the outer surface of the bowl. Hence the
need for thickness in the wall. Better a squat, thick-set pipe than
an ordinary one with little wood in it; better to have to scrape out
a pipe frequently than—as with my own eyes I have actually seen
done—get rid of what is supposed to be superfluous wood by burning it away with a red-hot poker or some other barbarous method
that ruins the wood and destroys its flavor. (See the drawing we

have below.) As we shall see, slight and frequent scraping modifies most agreeably the savor of a pipe.

The depth of the bowl, important as it is, depends in principle upon the kind of pipe.

The Bottom of the Bowl.   The shape of the bottom of the bowl can vary greatly. Without laying down the law in regard to any particular kind, we would counsel the reader to avoid the "indirect," as shown below, which gets choked, as well as the "flat," which causes too much charring, the drawing being lateral rather than terminal. As can be seen, there are no hard and fast

Indirect   *Direct*

rules, no inflexible canons to regulate the shape either of the exterior or the interior of the bowl; the preference of the smoker is the

chief criterion. For our own part we prefer the bulldog, with the
wall fairly thin at the point where the tobacco is lighted, thicker

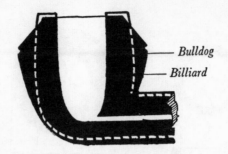

— *Bulldog*
— *Billiard*

where the combustion or smoldering attains its maximum, and
gradually tapering as it falls to the stem. By this design all superfluous wood is dispensed with—making it easier on the teeth—without
damage to the pipe itself. The bulldog is a sort of simplified billiard,
and not merely the product of a maker's whim, as its appearance
might lead one to suspect.

Caliber. Of two pipes made from the same briar root, a large
pipe will be better than a small one. They will not have the same
taste, e en though the wood be identical. This is because the
smaller, having thinner walls to the bowl, will get hot at once and
draw badly, while the larger will get only warm and will be generous. If we do not recommend small pipes it does not mean necessarily that they should be considered as bad in themselves, since
everything depends on the quality of the wood. What is in question is the absurdity of small pipes, especially of small briars. The
following are the principal reasons: Hardly is the pipe alight before the lower portion of the tobacco gets hot, and the moisture in
the whole fill is well on the way to boiling, whereas the superheating should only take place at the top of the bowl at the actual
point of lighting. In other words, the space reserved for combustion
being too limited, the pipe will give only a dozen or so agreeable
whiffs—just enough to make the smoker wish for more.

We are not unaware of the fact that certain smokers—and veterans at that—have a great weakness for a small pipe, not only because it is lighter—which is certainly all to the good—and easier to carry—which is not at all an advantage—but also, and this is most important, because it is pleasing to the eye when united to a gently curving stem and mouthpiece. Now in these pages we are not concerned with æsthetics but with the practical side of pipe smoking, and we refuse to equate the briar pipe with a natty tie or a smart pair of gloves. Our study is of the pipe as an entity. We do not consider it from the ornamental aspect, though it has inspired more than one painter. We must not, therefore, bring the pipe to us so much as ourselves go out in search of it, seeking to approach it—above all endeavoring to learn by what means it may be made to yield the maximum of enjoyment. What do its looks matter!

THE WOOD.   With a little practice it is easy to distinguish at a glance good wood from bad, an even grain from an irregular one, the very heart of the briar root from the more or less similar elements that surround it.

Botanists teach us that in general the root is composed of an outer sheath and a central cylinder formed of bunches of fibers called perfect and imperfect, the latter furnishing what, in the secondary structure, becomes the texture of the wood itself. Without pursuing this further, it is no bad thing to have an idea of what one is about when it comes to making a selection from some hundreds of specimens, each of which has its own identity; it is no bad thing to have some knowledge, even if it be somewhat hazy and partakes more or less of a sort of mythical mnemonic technique, the sort of thing that lingers in our minds from prep-school days— "What everyone ought to know," though one only knows it really when it has been forgotten. A man who is indifferent to Nature cannot make as judicious a choice of a pipe as one who takes an interest in the world around him.

It sometimes happens that in shops that make no claim to specializing in their wares one comes across pipes made of excellent wood but badly sawn or of otherwise defective manufacture. Other pipes may appear faultless but are made of wood which, from a first glance, can leave the expert eye with no doubt as to its ori-

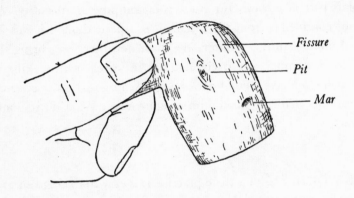

gin. We have already indicated the shady methods by which certain makers foist off pipes made of the outer wood of the root, the pericardium as it were; this may explain the subsequent appearance of those mysterious brown spots on pipes that appear almost perfect when bought, a failing which we illustrate in this drawing.

As a general rule very cheap briar pipes should be avoided. There are exceptional cases, of course, but they only go to make the rule. Inferior pipes are occasioned by bad turning in the lathe which affects the shape, by marks and blemishes, and by many indications invisible to the lay eye but patent to the professional at a glance. A practiced eye is necessary to perceive why some pipes are cheaper than others. One must know one's job, and the smoker's job is by no means the same as that of the maker. Not all pipe-makers are pipe smokers, and even if they were it would be impossible for them to sample all their wares. There are certain pipes of well-known makes that are worth nothing; on the other hand there are pipes with no trademark that are thrust aside in some dusty cupboard or upon the highest shelf in the shop which are of unique quality.

The best thing to do is to go to some craftsman pipemaker, preferably a small tobacconist in a country town, select a pipe in the rough, that is to say unpolished and unvarnished, and have the bowl mounted to your liking with a long, short, stout or slim stem of ebonite, horn or what you will. This is the best way to save oneself unpleasant surprises. You will recognize the authentic briar root by its color in the rough, a medium beige and fairly light. Only an exceptional degree of working upon the wood can produce that warm brown that is so satisfying to the eyes.

The grain of the wood—the *motif* as one might call it—appears either in longitudinal and transverse fibers (in the latter they should be close) or in the knots that may be grouped together here and there amongst the fibers. The quest for a particular sort of grain, such as a straight grain, is one for appearance's sake only. The original cutting of the root into cubes makes it rare to obtain in a single pipe one or other of these appearances of the grain exclusively; they are usually found together in fairly equal proportions. In any case, they have the same virtues and one is as good as the other.

The choice of a pipe is in great part a matter of flair. There is an ideal pipe—your ideal pipe—to which you turn instinctively and without hesitation; it will leave another smoker quite unmoved. The English and Americans, for instance, prefer a straight grain; the French are more appreciative of a good cut across the grain. The true smoker thinks only of the closeness of the grain, however it may be cut.

Some pipes are, apart from their own intrinsic qualities as utensils for smoking, pure marvels of nature—sometimes even of craftsmanship. We have seen two or three in which the bottom of the bowl was a base out of which arose a cluster of fibers that, as they ascended toward the brim, broke into countless tiny knots like so many bubbles. There were others in which the base of the bowl was a veritable mass of knots out of which endless fibers rose in straight and perfect regularity.

Knots, fibers, and other elements of the grain are all so many hieroglyphics that, when understood, speak to the professional eye just as Nature speaks to the trapper of wild animals or to the writer of eclogues. That is why it is imperative never to disregard certain rules, the first and foremost of which is: Look at the pipe in the unvarnished wood, so that even if the inspection be somewhat casual there can be no possibility of your being palmed off with a pipe in which holes in the bowl have been cunningly filled with putty or plastic, and concealed by coloring and varnish. It should always be borne in mind that the briar root has only one heart, so only a limited number of pipes can be made to an almost absolute perfection.

There are true pipe smokers and there are pipe collectors. Let us all beware lest in our cult of the briar root we become mere collectors. Some smokers assert that only a single pipe is needed. With due respect to their opinions, which are doubtless founded on careful consideration, we are not of this school. On the other hand we absolutely reject the opposite extreme. Whether one has one pipe or a hundred, the essential thing is so to select them that each is worthy of the rest, that a new pipe does not cause an old one to blush. Thus shall we prove ourselves worthy of our pipes.

Personally, we do not hesitate to affirm that it is the living appearance of the wood that determines our selection of a pipe, when the woody and cellular fibers seem condensed and knit together voluntarily, when the texture of the grain seems to defy the tool that shapes it. These filaments and little knots in the grain are the living image of the life of the plant; it is from them that arise those impalpable rings of pleasure that afford such ecstasy to the nostrils.

The French have a word for seasoning a pipe—*culotter;* Larousse defines this as "darkening a pipe by use." If the light color of the briar is not to your liking, rest assured that after a dozen or so smokes the bowl will have become sensibly darker. Moreover, it will have acquired a natural luster that is far nobler and more venerable than the gloss of any luxury varnish, for it is genuine patina. The hand that holds the pipe in the palm contributes to this metamorphosis; the man who buys a highly varnished article misses the joy of seeing it grow a richer brown from the caress of his hands.

"I smoke a pipe as brown as the breast of a little Negress," wrote the poet Francis Jammes.

This phrase, quoted from memory, will, we hope, lead the smoker to daydreams—in a good sense, naturally.

THE STEM AND MOUTHPIECE. The mouthpiece is the secondary member of a pipe; but this secondary member is so important a part of the whole that it needs a section to itself.

Material. The substance from which the mouthpiece is made would appear to be a matter of no importance except in so far as it adds to the enjoyment of the pipe; but this is not where its importance lies.

The ebonite or vulcanite mouthpiece has been adopted as a matter of convenience and comfort. This material is derived from rubber hardened by vulcanization. It is not so hard—and at the same time does not break so easily—as amber or one of the plastics, and it is more homogeneous than horn. In short, it is a substance perfectly adapted for the purpose, for it resists by reason of its suppleness the action of the teeth, without in any way damaging their enamel.

Amber is a luxury substance, belonging as much to the jeweler's shop as to the tobacconist's pipes. Its origin, or rather its history, makes a poem in itself that we cannot pass over in silence. It is most often of a characteristic color, known indeed as "yellow amber"—a familiar sight to the cigar smoker.

Amber is fossilized resin. Sometimes the remains of fossilized insects are met with when a lump of it is cut, and at one time this was considered a certain proof of the genuineness of the article, but Conan Doyle pointed out that there was an industry in London for making imitation amber and even of inserting imitation flies in it. This may or may not be true, it is more likely to have been so when amber cigar holders were more in fashion. This vegetable origin gives amber an individual interest that has always aroused curiosity in view of the diverse uses to which it can be put. It is formed of a combination of resinous oils, rich in carbon and containing a certain amount of bitumen. The color varies from a pale yellow to a hyacinth red. Amber is found principally along the Baltic coast of Prussia, near Memel and Königsberg. The Greeks obtained it from the shores of the Black Sea and called it "elektron"; from the phenomenon that occurred when it was rubbed briskly came our word "electricity." Amber is also found in Sicily and elsewhere. It dates from the tertiary period and comes from the vast forests of the pine known to botanists as *pinus succinfer,* from the Latin *succinum,* meaning amber. The most precious variety is of a dull, greenish-yellow, glassy in appearance and slightly clouded.

Ambergris, despite its name, which in French means "gray amber," has nothing whatever to do with true amber. It is a fatty substance excreted by the sperm whale and has a fragrant musky odor that makes it of great use to perfumers; it cannot be used for pipes or cigarette-holders.

Without pronouncing definitely for one or other of the substances already enumerated, we can most emphatically advise against a wood mouthpiece, even if it be compressed wood as in the illustration below. It becomes impregnated with saliva—and for this reason offers ever less resistance to the teeth—until at last it degenerates into a sort of pulp, nasty to the taste and offensive to the touch, unhealthy and requiring constant paring down

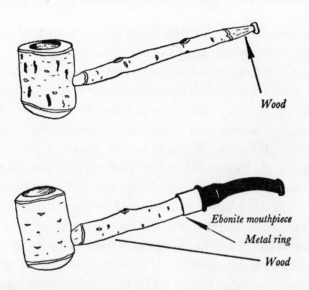

Wood

Ebonite mouthpiece
Metal ring
Wood

until the whole stem is reduced to nothing. The only remedy is to fit the pipe with an ebonite or other mouthpiece (which, for the reader's benefit, we show above), as was done with the gambier.

After some time ebonite ceases to resist moisture; it then turns a greenish gray in hue and is as unpleasant in appearance as it is in taste. At the first symptom of such a state of affairs preventive treatment is demanded with mineral soap or some other abrasive. This decay, however, happens only in very old pipes; nowadays pipes are immunized against it, provided, of course, that the ebonite is of the best quality. This, alas, is not always the case. As with horn, there is good ebonite and bad—or not so good. In a mouthpiece of inferior ebonite one can see as time goes on where the smoker's lips have caused a deterioration in the material. Naturally, this change is less evident with dry smokers than with wet.

It goes without saying that it is quite possible to renew or change the mouthpiece of a pipe. So long as the wooden part of the stem is not destroyed a smoker can have his pipe fitted with a new mouthpiece whenever it seems good to him to do so. In England, in the reign of the first Elizabeth, the pipe was made of a sort of nutshell which was circulated round the table, each guest having a mouthpiece of straw which he pushed into the hole at the base of the nut. Such a usage is still customary in the East.

Shape and Length. The gauge of a stem or mouthpiece is of no importance whatever; some smokers like a slender one, others prefer a thicker. It can be circular in section, square, triangular, etc., according to the shape of the pipe. The tendency is, however, toward a long, tapering shape combining pleasing lines with strength. In the matter of length, evidence goes to show that the curved shape is more rational than the straight, for the simple reason that from the former the smoke rises direct from the bowl to the nostrils, which not only furthers its enjoyment to the full but also affords less opportunity for it to become dispersed (see page 49), for there is always a considerable percentage of loss in smoking.

But here we find ourselves faced with a dilemma, for the distance between the pipe bowl and the smoker's nostrils must not be too restricted, as we find in the cutty or "nose-warmer" * which, so to speak, has no stem at all. This may be exemplified thus: You are not smoking yourself but you stand or walk by the side of or

---

* The "nose-warmer" must surely have made its first appearance at sea or in some country where the wind or other atmospheric conditions made proper pipe smoking impossible. The quid of tobacco probably came into usage for similar or other reasons. There is a regulation of 1684 in the French Navy to the effect that any sailor found smoking would be punished with eight days in irons and the loss of a month's pay. Another such order gave a captain authority to seize and have beaten with a stick any passenger found smoking in his ship.

behind someone smoking a pipe. Suddenly you find your sense of
smell—and indeed your personal pride—strangely excited by the
exceptionally delightful aroma of your friend's pipe. A most
heady, overpoweringly delicious smell is wafted to you and your
senses are captured by the most sumptuously violent emanation of
astounding intimacy, penetrating, farreaching, breathing the very
essence of things; and you are overwhelmed with chagrin that
among all your battery of pipes there is none possessing such
personality. Yet the probability is that your friend's pipe is in no
way superior to any of your own. The truth is that between the
bowl of his pipe and your nostrils there was just sufficient space to
allow the aroma to give out its maximum, to be at its ripest. In
that stretch of air, a sort of delayed chemical action was taking
place, unless it was just the cooling of the smoke when it left the
bowl. Whatever the reason, the fact remains. This phenomenon is
of everyday occurrence and is classic among smokers; the best
pipe is always someone else's.

But with a pipe, the taste and the aroma are indivisible; the
aroma alone is not enough for us, and the taste is not really complete, except when we ourselves are smoking. It is therefore best
to take an active, not passive, part.

Many people make the mistake of looking upon the long-
stemmed pipe as nothing but a sort of artistic whim, whereas it is

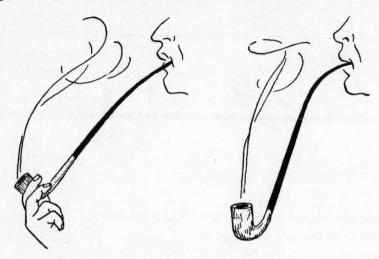

the fruit of a transcendent logic inherited from generations of smokers.

It is for reasons given above that we have the long, straight mouthpiece or stem issuing from the base of the bowl (illustrated above, left), as well as the long, curved—and better, doubly curved —mouthpiece shown on the right which permits the maximum of smoke to waft in the maximum of space at the minimum of distance. In addition to this, in the curved stem, such as that of the calabash, the smoke rises of its own volition. This shape possesses the additional advantage of allowing one to smoke in comfort while lying in bed. It should, however, be pointed out that by the law of gravity a curved pipe tends to choke up more often and requires scraping out more frequently.

One often finds an advocate of the straight stem lowering the bowl of his pipe without taking the mouthpiece from his teeth. What is his object in doing this? Make no mistake about it; he is just obeying the fundamental law of the curved stem. If he droops his pipe bowl it is to obtain a more direct effluence from the combustion of the tobacco and thus afford his nostrils full measure of the undispersed fragrance. It is the sovereign law of pleasure! Certain it is that if all one had to smoke during a whole day was a solitary pipeful of tobacco instead of a nice packet, one would become a really proficient smoker. That is what happened in France during the Occupation and for some years after—unless one had recourse to the cigarette for a speedier intoxication.

Needless to say, the stem and mouthpiece must be straight or curved according to the shape of the pipe itself. This, again, is a matter of taste. The ideal from our point of view would be a half-curved stem which would combine the advantages of all other types with certain particular virtues of its own.

The Mouthpiece Itself. The end, or bit, as it may be called, of the mouthpiece may be classed in two principal categories according to the orifice—the wide and the narrow. The general thickness of the mouthpiece containing the narrow orifice offers greater resistance to the bite of the smoker; the wide orifice entails less strain on the gums by spreading the tooth-hold over a larger area. The choice rests solely with the smoker, and depends largely on the disposition of his teeth and their condition, and the strength of his jaws.

The orifice of the bowl end of the stem is important. It ought not to be too wide or shreds of tobacco may get into it and choke

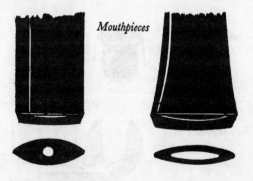

Mouthpieces

it, nor must it be too small, for then the pipe will not draw. A happy medium is essential. Let it be left to the maker to supply what he considers best, though at the same time it is well to inspect both the mouth end and the bowl end of the stem ourselves to make sure there is no defect, such as is so often found in clays.

A mouthpiece will often be large enough to allow the smoker to minimize the effect of the stream of smoke upon his tongue if he opens and widens the orifice with a penknife or some such tool.

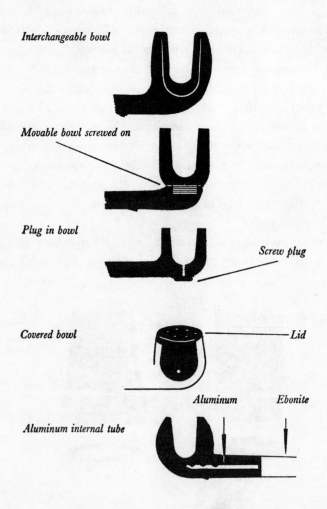

Interchangeable bowl

Movable bowl screwed on

Plug in bowl   *Screw plug*

Covered bowl   *Lid*

                                                    Aluminum   *Ebonite*

Aluminum internal tube

GENERAL REMARKS. During the operation of smoking it is permissible—even advisable—to hold the bowl of the pipe in one hand without removing the mouthpiece from the lips. This procedure, which is rational and at the same time restful, is possible even when out for a walk. It is the general practice of genuine smokers; but triflers and novices in the art of smoking a pipe seem to imagine that it is elegant to walk, pipe in mouth, with one hand in a trouser pocket and the other lightly dangling a pair of gloves. True, their pipes are as often as not unlighted, even empty of tobacco. A pipe does not make a man of the world any more than a cigarette does; it is when a man is smoking properly that he acquires a certain interest for others.

As we have seen, there is no such thing as the ideal pipe—the requisite conditions for making one cancel each other out; but there are several types that, put together, would make the perfect pipe. Opposite we depict in section a number of examples, the advantages of which, it will be seen, are not without relation to the stem and mouthpiece. They allow us to appreciate the attempts of pipemakers throughout the centuries to perfect the tobacco pipe, and initiate us into some of the mysteries of the pipe world with which this book is concerned.

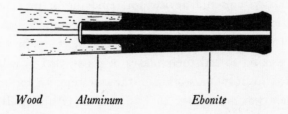

Wood   Aluminum   Ebonite

The internal stem illustrated in this diagram (the one above) is made of aluminum and has certain qualities and defects. Among the former is the extra strength given to the stem at its most easily broken part. Of the latter, the most important is that the aluminum tube fits so tightly against the wood that the absorption and filtering of the moisture of the tobacco by this wood is hindered. For this reason the pipe requires constant cleaning out. The ideal would consist in a ring of metal, as shown above, encircling the end of the wood stem. In this way absorption and filtering are only slightly hindered, while the pipe is made as strong as could be desired.

In conclusion, we would advise against a stem fitted too low into the base of the bowl, because of the task this base fills in filtering the tobacco when burning. This is especially applicable when the stem is of aluminum or some other metal. As a general rule, the less a pipe is made up of elements alien to the wood, the better chance it has of tasting and smoking to perfection. Whatever means may be taken to make it stronger, a pipe cannot but be fragile, and this should be an axiom ever in the smoker's mind. Indeed, that is why valuable pipes with a strong and often elegant case are usually avoided.

ANTI-NICOTINE CONTRAPTIONS

The various systems and devices for removing or preventing the accumulation of nicotine in the pipe have assumed such importance, and pipemakers have worked the subject up into such an abuse in seeking to sell their makes of pipes, that it will be far from useless to devote a section to the question. In former times the problem was not appreciated, or was solved naturally by the use of water, as in the narghile on page 16.

Let it be stated at once that the various systems now employed belong rather to the realm of advertising and publicity than to that of the pipe and pipe smoking. The picture of an enlarged pipe shown in section, depicting the working of one of these most complicated systems in much the same style as an anatomical diagram, is well calculated to induce the novice to imagine that he has at last discovered how to smoke without injuring his health. Pipes with a filter or some porous matter at the bottom of the bowl have had, and still have their vogue. But notwithstanding their scientific appearance we ought not to be carried away by a fallacious publicity too often reminiscent of a huckster in the market-place of a Saturday night. The classic procedure of the quack doctor is familiar enough: to make out that the ailment is worse than it is, so that the cure shall appear all the more marvelous. Let us smoke our pipe by all means, but let us not be tricked by such nonsense.

Tobacco was formerly considered a drug; more than a hundred weighty treatises and books were written denouncing it.* On its introduction into France a police ordinance prohibited its use except by apothecaries on pain of a fine of 80 Paris francs, or some 35s. of English money, in those days a considerable sum. Louis XIII dealt it a hard blow, and Urban VIII went so far as to excommunicate all who used it. Three monks, we are told, who were taken in the act of smoking were arraigned and executed. In Asia Minor the Sultan Achmet IV decreed that all smokers should have their noses and ears cut off, and the edict was put into force; his example was followed by the Tsar Michael of Russia and the King of Prussia. Even later, toward the close of the eighteenth century, the Vienna police had orders to fire on anyone seen smoking, whether a pipe or a cigarette. Danger of fire was the pretext usually invoked for these stringent measures. It reminds us of the

* Among the works on this subject we might mention Doctor Pauli and the surgeon Borry, whose names are long since forgotten, and Doctor Boussiron, whose name soon will be, author of *Concerning Tobacco and its influence upon the health and morals of man.* In favor of tobacco, from a documentary angle, we find the philosopher, physician and hymn-writer Menander or Neander of Bremen (1650–80) who wrote a treatise on "Tabaccology" and his contemporaries Mouard and Eberhard; Contugi wrote *Non ergo nocet cerebro tabacum,* which created a sensation at the time.

rules against the "nose-warmer" as already cited on page 48.

These measures which seem to us decidedly drastic were less so in those earlier times, for smoking had become the habit to an astounding degree and was actually a public scandal, priests even approaching the altar to say Mass pipe in mouth. Urban VIII authorized beadles in churches to confiscate tobacco boxes, though it should not be assumed that this was in any way related to the fact that they were usually made of gold or silver.

When the State showed its claws in France and declared a monopoly of tobacco, the question of the stuff being a poison, or a drug, or a stupifacient, was relegated to the background and no more was heard of it. With his innate logic, the French taxpayer is forced to conclude that all those noxious elements that were once so inimical to public health have not only lost their danger but have become actually beneficial now that smoking has become a profitable concern to the exchequer. Opium and cocaine now occupy the evil place once filled by tobacco in the early seventeenth century, but—we are speaking of France and French history, for a tobacco monopoly has never been established in Britain—since the privilege of making and selling tobacco was taken over by the State in 1674, any writing against the habit of smoking has been considered a lapse of taste. We must, however, remain logical at all costs—though still taxpayers—and take it that the campaign against opium and cocaine is, historically speaking, just as baseless as that ancient one against tobacco. It will be enough for the State—always the philanthropist—to take over a monopoly of narcotics for us to find posters at every street corner advocating their use and lauding to the skies one or other of their natures. And all for the common good.

To return to our systems. We do not deny the utility of anti-nicotine methods nor their value, nor even their efficiency; it is not our task to settle such problems. The use (not the abuse) of tobacco is not harmful. How many persons have we not known who, accustomed to smoking a dozen cigarettes a day, got it into their heads that it was ruining their health and took to denicotinized cigarettes—and smoked double the number. Beyond the fact that the suppression of the alkaloid—in the case of cigarettes— robs the burning tobacco of its aroma, these persons have affected the medical aspect of the case not one whit. They have worked themselves into a state of nerviness for no purpose, and have been robbed of much pleasure, for the source of the aroma lies in the camphor or nicotine in tobacco; without this nicotine the stuff is no better than hay.

If a smoker does not spit, says Doctor Joly, his stomach absorbs a considerable quantity of nicotine and ammonia. So be it; on the other hand if he does spit he loses the ferments contained in tobacco, ferments that are a direct aid to digestion.

All this goes to prove the futility of meddling with the natural course of smoking. It is far better for the smoker to adopt a regime suited to his needs and capacity. The better one knows oneself the better one's state of health.

All gadgets—generally made of aluminum on account of its lightness—are a useless and perverse luxury; they only serve to spoil smoking, to make the pipe "grumble," to obstruct the channel of the stem and thereby produce a host of other troubles by preventing the wood portion of the stem from fulfilling its proper

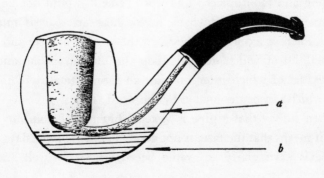

function. What we call the foot of the pipe (see page 57, *b*), although actually belonging neither to the bowl nor the stem, performs a capital function in the chemistry of combustion. It is that part of the pipe where the lowest portion of the tobacco is most moist and where the smoke, being drawn in, makes a curve in its progress to the mouth. Thus *a* and *b* both act as a filter or even regulator. To add a metal part to this is to nullify or at any rate, to spoil this effect.

"Anti-nicotine" pipes give an after-taste of stale nicotine that no true smoker can mistake; indeed, they can be "spotted" by the smell alone. What is to be said, then, of the taste of bubbling nicotine, the disgusting stench of which but serves to emphasize the fact that no pipe ought ever to be smoked after it has got hot? It is this smell that has always set us against the so-called Alsatian pipes, particularly those confected with a whole battery of aluminum "anti-nicotine" gadgets. The naturally healthy, light aroma of the tobacco cannot get through, it is completely and utterly poisoned. This goes to prove that excessive filtering is not only undesirable but ruinous to the taste.

This appears to be the moment to define as clearly as possible what smokers mean by this word "taste."

When one speaks of the "taste" of a pipe, what is meant is the taste of the smoke released from the burning tobacco and rising from the bowl, rather than that of the smoke which passes through the stem and mouthpiece. The word "smell" would not be comprehensive enough to describe it, for here an analysis must be made. There is a difference between the papillæ of taste and those of smell, all of which depend upon the mucous membrane, the sensitivities of which interpenetrate to form a totality of impressions which can be designated by the word "taste."

When we say that a pipe is "sweet" but that it does not smell nice, it means that the taste is not good. There are some days when a pipe is particularly enjoyable because it draws well and the smoke is delicious. This really depends in turn on the general state of the smoker's health. For example, a cold in the head is bad for conducting the odoriferous properties in the smoke; in cases of serious illness the organism cannot tolerate tobacco. The nasal and olfactory mucous membranes play a large part in the sensory faculties of the smoker; they form the seat of the taste and in some degree act the part of an anti-nicotine filter. It is not, therefore, the mouth alone that takes part in the act of smoking; it is the entire organism.

We thus arrive at the conclusion that a pipe having none of these systems and gadgets but which is cleaned often and carefully will eliminate just as much nicotine as is needful without harming the health of the smoker or depriving him of the pleasure he enjoys in smoking. But little experience of pipe smoking is sufficient to expose the futility of such engines; indeed one would imagine that some of them were designed for some purpose quite other than smoking tobacco. These affairs may be useful for scraping out the pipe; but the first thing to do when buying a pipe fitted with such gadgets is to take them all out (always supposing them to be removable, which is not always the case).

It is really a remarkable thing that craftsmen and manufacturers seem to have found in the various parts of so simple an object as the pipe an apparently limitless field for their ingenuity; patent medicine quacks and charlatans in general have nothing on them, as the saying is, in this connection. As the meerschaum has had portions of a briar added to it, and the briar has been dressed up with bits of copper, so someone has invented—or alleged he has invented—a hydraulic or water pipe, a gas-retort pipe, a condenser pipe, a refrigerator pipe, and heaven knows what else! A pipe on the principle of the pump was followed by one devised on the siphon system. The varieties of filter pipes, with cotton-wool tubes and anti-nicotine pads are beyond reckoning. Tobacco smoke has been passed through all sorts of substances with filtering or anti-

nicotine properties—charcoal, asbestos and the like—sometimes
introduced into the bowl, sometimes in the stem or mouthpiece;
mineral and vegetable substance alike have been called into use.

One thing is certain, when the products of combustion are sepa-
rated and collected in these ways they are poisonous, more poisonous than when in their normal condition. Doing violence to Nature
rebounds in violence to oneself. Nature does not sell her goods,
she bestows them and is quite indifferent as to what use we make
of them. Man should learn to enjoy and use them, not to abuse
them.

We have written at some length about systems of denicotiniza-
tion in order to get rid of the subject once and for all. They have
nothing to do with the pipe. Only the water-filter, on the principle
of the narghile, appears to us as being efficient and worthy of
consideration. Unfortunately it is not easily transportable, as is
seen in this drawing. The best pipe manufacturers have adopted

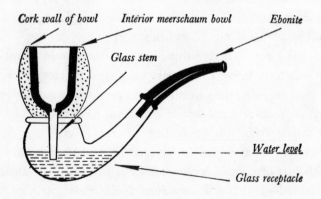

Cork wall of bowl   Interior meerschaum bowl   Ebonite

Glass stem

Water level

Glass receptacle

various very simple measures whereby their pipes may be easily
cleaned and the smoke more or less filtered; but once again a
word of warning must be given, for the introduction of the end
of the ebonite mouthpiece into the delicate and fragile wood of the

stem makes breaking very easy. The bowl and the stem and mouth-piece are not really adapted to one another, some sort of binding tape or the like outside the stem is what is really needed. In the choice of a pipe a careful inspection of this joint should be made; it is even advisable during the first few smokes not to push the ebonite firmly into the wood stem lest the heating of one or both may distort the pipe.

Let us away with all anti-nicotine pipe devices; by their very name they stand self-condemned. It is a concession even to intro-duce such an uncongenial substance as ebonite into the wood. Na-ture and manufacture do not go well together.

CHOICE OF TOBACCO

There are three kinds of tobacco:

>   Snuff, *tabacum pulveratum.*
>   Chewing tobacco, *tabacum aptum mundi.*
>   Smoking tobacco, *tabacum fumicum.*

Although in times of great distress and dearth the first two may be smoked in a pipe, we will here confine our remarks to the properties of the last.

DEFINITIONS AND PROPERTIES.   Tobacco is a plant the historical origin of which is as difficult to ascertain as the ety-mology of its name. According to the missionary Barthélémy de las Cases, a contemporary of Columbus, the name comes from the fact that the plant, which at that time grew wild and underwent no sort of preparation, was wrapped in a dry leaf which the In-dians called "tabacos." *

* Las Cases wrote in 1527: "The Indians burn a herb of which they inhale the smoke with delight. This herb is wrapped in a dried leaf rolled in the

In Central America, however, where it probably originated it is called "petum" from a Guarani word, and this has traveled to the Orient as "tutum" and to Brittany and France as "petun" or "tutun." † Later it took pseudonyms too numerous to retail, though "tobacco" is the name now known in every country and language. These various appellations were the subject of controversy in France when it came to imposing a tax. In 1760 the High Court determined to make every name for tobacco synonymous in order to forestall tax evasion. Thanks to the botanist Joseph de Tournefort (1656-1708) the name of nicotine has always perpetuated Jean Nicot (1530-1600) who introduced the herb to France, and that name was accepted by the High Court.

Twelve species of tobacco are known to botanists, but only a few are cultivated. Tobacco belongs to the Solanaceæ family. The plant grows to a height of some two feet, with flowers in clusters or panicles. Two kinds especially should be distinguished:

Nicotiana rustica, with yellow flowers and large leaves, grown in Brazil, Asia Minor, Hungary and certain districts of France.

Nicotiana tabacum, with red or pink flowers. There are more than thirteen varieties of this, cultivated in Havana,

---

manner of those tubes children make at Whitsunday out of paper. The Indians light one end and suck or draw in at the other, breathing in the smoke which produces a sort of lethargy of the whole body that degenerates into a sort of drunken stupor. They assert that in this condition they feel no fatigue of any sort. These rolls or 'tabacos' as they call them, are in use among our colonists; and when they were reprimanded for indulging in such a bad habit they answered that it was impossible to break themselves of it. I do not know what pleasure or profit they get from it."

The word "tobacco" belongs to the Carib dialect. It is not known whether the word describes the plant or the apparatus for smoking it. This Carib word is employed in Havana where "Chupar un tabago" means to smoke a cigar.

† "Petun" is the word employed by the Indians in Florida; according to Raleigh the North American Indians called it Uppwoc.

Malaya, Maryland, Ohio, Kentucky, Turkey, Brazil, Sumatra, Java, the Far East and parts of France and Algeria.

The best tobaccos are those least charged with nicotine. Thus Havana, Manila, Sumatra, Turkey and Asia Minor produce the lightest and most odoriferous kinds. Oriental tobaccos are lighter in color and better adapted for better cigars. Light-colored tobacco deteriorates sooner than the other; this can be perceived by the patches that appear after a certain time on the paper in which cigarettes are rolled, or on the packet of loose tobacco. It is for this reason that such tobacco is always packed in metal-lined boxes, and sold in silver paper.

The species Nicotiana (family Solanaceæ to which belong the tomato, aubergine, potato, pimento, datura, petunia and sundry poisonous plants containing alkaloids employed in pharmacy) is very little cultivated in Europe. Its nature and properties vary according to the original habitat, the nature of the soil in which it is being grown, and the method of cultivation.

Nicotine was first isolated in 1809 by the chemist N. L. Vauguelin (1763-1829). Its chemical composition and its proportion in tobacco was established by Théophile Schloesing (1856-1930)—a somewhat uncertain proportion to define as it depends upon the preparation of the leaves before being dealt with commercially. However, it is known that even after preparation the American, Dutch and Oriental tobaccos contain the least nicotine.

The tobacco plant is noxious; it acts on the intestinal canal and the pituitary membrane, causing vomiting. In small doses it can be used as a purge. In powder form it will cleanse the mucous membrane of serous matter. When chewed it makes an excellent antiseptic. The oil extracted from it is the source of the aroma. Maleic and citric acids can also be obtained. But from a commercial point of view the most interesting thing about it is its smoke.

HISTORY.　How can we come to any agreement on the date of the discovery of tobacco when even the discovery of America is a point in dispute? And what, in fact, *is* discovery? Are the discoverers those who have discovered themselves and thereupon set out to discover other peoples who neither want to be discovered nor to discover others? Is it the "civilized" person who discovers the "savage," or the "savage" who discovers the "civilized" man who has put himself to the trouble of coming to discover him? It may well cause a smile when one thinks that the pride of nations can find little other outlet than in constant "discovery."

According to recent historians it is now established that the first European smoker was the Spaniard Rodrigo de Jerez, who sailed with Columbus and brought back tobacco from Cuba to Spain in 1498. Other historians, however, of no less standing, assert that it was Hernandez de Toledo who imported it from Yucatan to Portugal in 1520. Yet others allege that a Spanish hermit named Roman Pane had revealed its existence to Europe nearly a century earlier. Murray, who denies its American origin, states that the knowledge of tobacco came to Europe from the East in the fifteenth century. His theory is based on the narrative of a traveling merchant named Chardin who, while residing in Persia, found that tobacco had been naturalized there not from the fifteenth but from the thirteenth—or even the twelfth—century. Even more audaciously, other historians assert that tobacco was in remote ages employed as a narcotic in certain parts of Europe and Asia. Vestiges of roots, they say, have been found in the Ardennes; but there is nothing really conclusive in this when we recollect that Magnesius, protagonist of the American origin school, has an explanation in the fact that seed can have been carried on the wind from the New World to the Old. The German naturalist and Chinese explorer Pallas (1741-1811) says that among the Mongol tribes having relations with China, smoking was so common a custom that the tobacco pouch attached to the belt was an indispensable item of clothing, and that it was these Mongol pipes that the Dutch took as models for their own. Pipes are found in Chinese sculptures dating from a very remote period, and their form is practically identical with that of the pipes the Chinese smoke to this day.

Theories such as these run contrary to that of a European origin. We have not got much further in our researches into the problem of the origin of the pipe, unless it be that we have once again come back to the fact that (apart from any question of tobacco) men have always smoked. So to what end do all these arguments tend? Plants die out and vanish even as races of mankind do, even as certain species of animals have done. What is there to prove that our caveman ancestors did not know tobacco? The plant may well have disappeared in the passage of the ages—it may have been lost to us though it survived elsewhere.

In the year 1492 Christopher Columbus "discovered" America. On October 12 he landed on an island called by the natives Guanahani, and took solemn possession of it in the names of the sovereigns of Castile, rechristening it the island of San Salvador. Historians are not agreed as to which of the five Bahama Islands it was. Setting sail southward he next steered for a large island called by the natives Cuba. He did not rename this, as in the case of Guanahani; he landed there on October 28. It was then that a converted Jew named Luis de Torres, whom the navigator had taken with him as an interpreter by reason of his familiarity with Hebrew, Chaldean and Arabic, was told to make his way into the interior of the island and make contact with the natives through the medium of one or other of those languages. The proficiency of the native Cubans in Hebrew, Chaldean or Arabic is not recorded, but it is through Luis de Torres that we learn that the people of the island carried in their hands a piece of burning charcoal, with herbs, and took in the smell of the latter by means of "catapults," which they called "tabacos." Where did the term come from? Was it from the island of Tobago or the town of that name? Sailors are not the men to bother about such questions as that. Having explored the country others confirmed the Jew's statements, reporting that the Indians of both sexes introduced into their nostrils a double-branched cigar holder in shape like a child's catapult. They held in their hands a sort of burning brand of some herb, of which they inhaled the smoke. This must have been in some sort the origin of the cigar. The herb was called "cohiba" and the burning brand "tabaco." The part has been taken for the whole, and instead of talking of "cohiba" we talk of "tobacco."

But historians are not agreed even on this theory. Tobacco is indigenous to Florida, and the Spaniards discovered it in the Gulf of Mexico, on the shores of the Bay of Campeche. As mentioned earlier, the Spaniards and Portuguese found it in the province of Tabasco, Yucatan. Hence the name, say they.

Besides the mariners of Columbus, those of Vespucci, Cortez and Magellan brought samples of the herb back to Europe. It was at Lisbon, in a private garden, that the first tobacco was grown in Europe. In 1518 Cortez brought back some seeds for the Emperor Charles V; they were sown broadcast and from that day onwards tobacco was cultivated in the Iberian peninsula.

In face of all these theories Jean Nicot would seem not to be in the picture as the man who introduced tobacco to France; but Tournefort has given his name immortality by employing it in the botanical nomenclature of the plant. Without this Jean Nicot's memory would not have survived, for his claim to the honor of introducing it has been contested. A Cordelier friar named André Thevet, one of the friends of the poets of the Pléiade and a great traveler, is a self-appointed candidate for the distinction. In 1556, some four years earlier than Nicot's introduction of the plant, Thevet brought from Brazil some seeds that he offered to the King under the name of "cosoba"—a name that he subsequently changed to "angoulmousin," in memory of his native town of Angoulime.

"I can claim for myself," he writes in one of his books, "to have been the first to bring the seed of this plant into France, to have sown it, and to have named the herb 'angoulmousin.' Some ten years after I had returned from that distant land an individual who had never so much as set foot in travel gave it his name."

But Thevet, in turn, must have been unaware that in 1542 the Saint-Malo navigator, Jacques Cartier, introduced "angoulmousin" into the north of France. Cartier was the first European to make his way up the St. Lawrence, in the course of one of his voyages to Canada; in his narrative of explorations he gives details of the plant and its use by the aborigines. "They possess," he says, "a certain herb by which they lay great store. They carry a certain amount of it in a little bag hanging round their necks. They make use of a little piece of hollow wood, resembling a whistle, and place the dry or even powdered herb in one end of this tube, the other end being in the mouth. Upon the herb they place a lighted charcoal, inhale the smoke, and puff it out again, their nostrils performing the office of chimneys."

All of which being duly stated, we still come back to the year 1560 when Jean Nicot, ambassador from the French King Francis II to Sebastian, King of Portugal, received from a Flemish merchant named Damien de Goes, who had just come from Florida, an herb that stained like ink and gave forth a heavy smoke. Damien de Goes showed Nicot how it was used, and the latter presented a few leaves to the Grand Prior of Lisbon. This was looked upon as a veritable discovery and the plant was called from this occasion, the Grand Prior's Herb. Returning to France, Nicot took some seed and a few leaves back with him to Court and presented his precious herb to Queen Catherine de' Medici, the King's mother, whence it was called Ambassador's Herb. Migraine or sick headache was prevalent in the royal circles, so Nicot made them take tobacco in a powdered form not unlike snuff, "as a remedy for the brain." As was only right and proper, the whole

Court followed suit, and before long all Paris began to use—and eventually abuse—the Queen's Herb.

From that time onward tobacco enjoyed a great vogue, principally as a medicament. It was taken mixed with aromatic herbs; infusions were employed as enemas for intestinal ailments. In the meantime it found its way to Italy through Cardinal Santa Croce and Niccoló Tornabuoni, Papal legates at the Court of Sebastian —whence even another name came to it, Santa Croce's Herb. It is popularly said to have been introduced into England by Sir Francis Drake, and into Ireland by Sir Walter Raleigh who, in 1593, made plans for its cultivation. It soon spread to the rest of England and to Scotland.

But here we embroil ourselves in fresh controversial matter; for if it is admitted that Raleigh introduced tobacco to Ireland in 1593, he must have taken the seed from the Low Countries and not from England, whither Drake had brought it from Virginia. This would make the Low Countries the first locality in Europe to become acquainted with the plant, notwithstanding the separate claims of Cartier and Thevet. On the other hand, it is known that England received it direct from Brazil in 1585, and that it was introduced by her into Turkey about 1600.

These controversies would be of little matter were it not for the wholly fallacious contention that it was in England and not in France that tobacco was first known, and that Drake forestalled Nicot by some years. We have already said enough about Nicot to be exonerated from any imputation of partiality if we withstand this contention with all our might. The earliest date we can find for the introduction of the herb into England is 1585. Its discovery here was described by James I in 1619, whereas Jean Nicot had taken it to France sixty years earlier, in 1560. In 1690, as we have seen, the botanist Tournefort called the new substance "nicotiane" in honor, as he said, of its immortal introducer Jean Nicot. But the name survived only in scientific circles. As

Fontanelle observes: "Misfortunes happen even to the names of plants, as witness nicotiane, now known only as 'tobacco.' "

Meanwhile the plant pursued its own course. Contemporary botanists such as Charles de l'Ecluse and Rembert Dodonoeus estimated that its cultivation was worth some 100,000 florins a year in the Low Countries alone. Not only in France, where the fashion of taking it as snuff was started by Queen Catherine de' Medici, but in Belgium and even Russia the highest society, followed by the middle classes, were swept up in a veritable frenzy of tobacco. In 1572 a book appeared under the title *Instruction sur l'herbe pétun, dite en France l'Herbe à la Reine ou Medicis* (Instruction on how to use the herb Petun, known in France as Queen's or Medici Herb). At the outset it was used only remedially, but before long it was being smoked; by the nobles, we are told, in silver pipes.

This craze necessarily led to reaction. Some physicians declared that the plant was harmful. Disputes arose between learned men. James I of England launched a malediction against it in his *Counterblaste to Tobacco* and declared that all usage of this noxious habit should be extirpated. He called it a "stinking herb," notwithstanding Sir Walter Raleigh's—and Queen Elizabeth's—desire to encourage its cultivation in England and Ireland. These anathemas uttered from the highest levels had their repercussions throughout Europe. As we have seen, Urban VIII launched his excommunication; Tsar Michael Feodorovich threatened with the knout anyone found smoking, his nose to be cut off on a repetition of the crime, and incorrigible offenders to be beheaded. In 1650 the prohibition in Russia became even more severe after an epidemic of fires in the capital. History—or maybe legend—relates that a smoker fell asleep with a pipe in his mouth "and set fire to his own house and the entire quarter of the city." The story would have been more plausible if it had been a cigarette, but a pipe is far less dangerous to the public safety. In Turkey the Sultan

Amurath IV issued his firman against smoking on the strength of a verse in the *Koran* condemning drunkenness. Abbas I, Shah of Persia, ordered that snuff-takers should have their noses cut off, and smokers their lips; one would imagine that in Persia the habit of chewing *tabacum aptum mundi* would become prevalent, for Abbas threatened no punishment for chewing a quid. Mohammed IV personally supervised the carrying out of anti-tobacco decrees and took pains to catch smokers in the act, having each one hanged with a pipe stuck through his nose and a roll of tobacco hung round his neck. We are not told whether the pipe was alight, or if the tobacco was straight cut. In Transylvania an ordinance of 1688 decreed that anyone growing tobacco should have his goods confiscated, and anyone caught smoking it should be fined from 200 to 300 florins. In England Henry VIII was content with threatening smokers with the birch, while Elizabeth confiscated pipes and tobacco boxes throughout the realm—with especial prohibition against snuff-taking in church—measures that, as usual, resolved themselves into a tax, in this case 2*d.* per pound of tobacco.

If tobacco has had its persecutors it has not lacked for advocates. The Polish Jesuits brought out a book entitled *Antimisocapnos* in reply to the treatise of James I of England. This work contained a defense of the herb, the fathers having from the first appreciated the error of giving it an anti-religious significance. The Bremen physician named Neander, whom we have already mentioned, published his *Tabakologie*. Raphael Thorius (d. 1625), an English physician, devoted to its praise a Latin poem entitled *Hymnus tabaci* (1610); Thomas Willis (1621-75), one of the earliest physicians to diagnose diabetes, prescribed tobacco as one of the most effectual narcotics.

Under the impulse of these courageous advocates European opinion began to swing in favor of the plant. Peter the Great declared himself for it openly. Other exalted personages followed his example. Governments seized the opportunity to change their tactics. Notwithstanding the prohibition issued by Louis XIII (himself a snuff-taker), his minister Cardinal Richelieu conceived the idea of making the treasury profit from the infatuation of the populace by imposing a tax of 30 sous a pound on all imported tobacco. A paternal government justified this imposition by saying that too cheap tobacco was prejudicial to the health of the people, so steps had to be taken to put matters right. Cash, please!

In Britain the laws and regulations against tobacco had never been really strict nor harshly enforced, and the habit of hard smoking flourished. About the mid-seventeenth century a French visitor to England wrote: "The supper being finished they set on the table half a dozen pipes and a packet of tobacco for smoking, which is a general custom as well with women as with men, who think that without tobacco one cannot live in England because they say, it dissipates the evil humors of the brain. When the children go to school they carry in their satchel a pipe which their mother took care to fill early in the morning, it serving them instead of breakfast." Some years later the old cynic Ned Ward wrote in his *London Spy* (1698) of a visit to Fleet Street: "Now we have a rare opportunity of replenishing our boxes with a pipe of fine tobacco; for the greatest retailer of that commodity lives on the other side of the way . . . so we entered the smoky premises of the famous fumigator. There a parcel of ancient worshipers of the wicked weed were seated, wrapped up in Irish blankets, to defend their withered carcasses from the malicious winds that only blow on old age and infirmity. There was no talk amongst them, but puff was the period of every sentence, and what they said was as short as possible, for fear of losing the pleasure of a whiff, as, 'How d'ye do?' *puff*. 'Thank ye' *puff*. 'Is the weed good?' *puff*. 'Excellent.' *puff*. 'What o'clock?' *puff* etc." It is of some interest to know that the shop patronized by Ned Ward was that of Benjamin Howes, at the corner of Shoe Lane, where he sold "old, mild,

sweet-scented Virginia tobacco for 20*d*. either large cut, small
cut, or long cut . . . Spanish in the roll for 8*s*. a pound and
Spanish and Virginia mixed for 3*s*. a pound."

The history of tobacco being so uneventful in Britain it may be
worth while to follow the course of legislation, or rules and regulations, as they developed in France.

In 1635 a regulation by the Lieutenant of Police in Paris restricted to apothecaries the sale of tobacco, and then only on a
physician's prescription. In certain towns tobacco figured among
the goods upon which the octroi or local excise was charged; 5 sous
a pound was the rate at Marseilles and some other places, and the
sum thus obtained went to the upkeep of the hospitals, the building
of churches or simply to relieve the local finances. In 1667 a
higher duty was put on tobacco imported from Virginia than on
imports from the French West Indies. Once this import duty had
been paid, free traffic in tobacco was allowed throughout the country. It was at this time that home-grown tobacco first made its appearance in any quantity. As it was free of import duty, cultivation of the plant flourished in many parts of central and southern
France; but in spite of this competition with the home producer,
the import duties were not relaxed.

In 1674 Colbert put the situation right by making a monopoly
of tobacco, though he was not the actual originator of the idea, for
it had already been adopted in Castile and León some forty years
earlier, as also by the Venetian Republic, the States of the Church,
Portugal and the Archduchy of Austria. Russia followed suit in
1697, then Italy, Spain, Prussia and certain other European countries. Up to the French Revolution of 1789, which gave complete
freedom to anyone to cultivate tobacco and deal in it, a monopoly
was the order of things in most countries.

In 1730 the monopoly was leased to the French West Indies
Company, and it was under their management that matters were
put on a purely business footing; which means to say that the

financial advantages were in favor of the Company. It has been computed that out of 72,000,000 francs paid in tax annually by the consumers, no more than 24,000,000 found its way to the Exchequer. Big Business levied an enormous tribute on the trade, and colossal fortunes were made. Officials succeeded in restricting the cultivation of French-grown tobacco in order to swell the amount that had to be imported from other sources. As we have said, the Revolution abolished the organization thus set up, but some economists, such as Necker, declared themselves in favor of the old order. But notwithstanding the urgent needs of the treasury and Mirabeau's ironic remark that although the State had declared the equality of men it had not reached the point of declaring the equality of plants, the monopoly was abolished by the Decree of 20-27 March 1791.

This era of complete liberty gave a great fillip to the home grower of tobacco, but it did not suffice to lower the price. After a while consumers were unanimous in denouncing such tobacco as was available as atrocious, and they demanded a return to the old monopolist regime. The trade had got into the hands of a few families who made vast fortunes by selling adulterated stuff, mixing into the already inferior tobacco powdered tan, the leaves of various trees, lime blossom and even hay. To these were added bad alcohol, poor quality drugs, and even vitriol, on the pretext of giving the tobacco body. Men such as these were worse even than the old monopolist merchants, and they made even greater fortunes. When the Revolution had taken its course, a wiser government imposed taxes and instituted a proper Regie or Excise Office to manufacture and deal with the whole question of tobacco.

One night during the winter of 1810, we are told by Maxime du Camp in his curious *Souvenirs littéraires,* in the course of a ball at the Tuileries, Napoleon noticed a woman so covered with diamonds that he demanded to know who she could be. He was told that she was the wife of a tobacco merchant. A few days later the tobacco monopoly was re-introduced in a decree drafted by the Emperor himself, and the regulations made by him—as in so many other matters in France—have been but little changed from his day to our own.

CULTIVATION. Tobacco grows naturally in tropical countries. It is found in a wild state in both American continents, China, Persia, Egypt, the Cape and Australia. In Brazil it flourishes all the year round and the root will last a dozen years or so. The plant does not flourish so well in temperate climates, and cultivation then demands considerable care. It requires a rich soil, nitrate fertilizers, dung, regular watering and sunshine. According to Schlossing clayey siliceous soils suit the plant best.

A great number of varieties are found. Among the ornamental types are the *Nicotiana affinis,* with white flowers, the so-called Giant tobacco plant with purple flowers, and the sort whose arborescent stem attains a height of some five or six feet, with greenish-yellow flowers in clusters. Some of these varieties give out a strong perfume and are so graceful that they adorn garden beds and borders.

In addition to the flower of the tobacco plant there is the fruit, which contains very fine seeds from which oil can be extracted. It is possible to cultivate all kinds of tobacco in parts of France and southern Europe but it is illegal to grow even single roots in cottage gardens in some districts. In Britain there are few regulations; apart from certain excise formalities, the cultivation and curing of tobacco for one's own use is permitted.

As we have seen, in addition to smoking tobacco there are two other sorts—snuff (*tabacum pulveratum*) and chewing tobacco (*tabacum aptum mundi*). Snuff is compounded of leaves of Virginia tobacco 18 per cent, locally grown leaves 74 per cent and throw-outs 8 per cent. Snuff of the best quality contains 5 per cent of special Virginia and other special tobacco. The composition can be yet further refined by mingling with various aromatic elements other than tobacco. It takes seventeen months to prepare ordinary snuff and more than twenty for select Virginia quality.

There are several varieties of chewing tobacco: fine plug, coarse plug, and "carrots." The plugs take the form of a twist of tobacco rolled into a cylinder; the "carrots" are pressed twists in the shape of that vegetable. These tobacco rolls can be chewed, smoked as cigars, or taken as snuff if ground up. They can also be packed in a pipe. The less coarse kinds are made of full-bodied leaves, while coarse plug and "carrots" contain a small mixture of some such leaf as Virginia or Kentucky; molasses or other sugar products are always used in preparing chewing tobacco.

PREPARATION.   So long as it is quite dry the tobacco leaf can be smoked without any sort of preparation; but it burns badly, is acrid to the taste, and leaves a thick dottle or residue unburned at the bottom of the bowl. The tobacco of commerce undergoes a lengthy preparation.

Sowing takes place in March, and the harvest should be in August or the early days of September. Soon after the seedlings appear they are thinned to a regular distance apart to ensure large leaves that shall be fully charged with nicotine. When these leaves have attained maturity they are gathered one by one and hung up by the stem to dry in a shed, loft or some other dry and dark place. When they are dry, which is shown by the stems becoming brittle, the leaves are sorted according to their size and quality, and packed in bundles of fifty, known as "hands." The tobacco then undergoes a period of fermentation which destroys some of the nicotine, after which the leaves are compressed into balls before going forward to the factory.

The next process consists in stripping off the stalk. The leaf is then moistened and thoroughly scoured in water containing a quantity of bay salt, which acts as a detergent and prevents a desiccation that might otherwise set in; for the plant is a sort of barometer, and in dry weather will easily crumble to powder at the slightest shock. This washing makes the leaves so supple that they can be cut up without being spoiled. At the same time the leaves are laid one upon another with the same side of each uppermost.

When the leaves are cleansed and properly laid in this way, they are sliced according to the cut of the tobacco required, and there are many cuts possible. The tobacco is then roasted to prevent any fermentation that might occur, which would change the quality of its aroma. This roasting at 140° F. destroys all fermentation and gives the tobacco its familiar curly appearance. It is then taken to a drying room at 68° F. where it is subjected to a current of cold air. The last operation consists in picking over the tobacco by hand and removing any knots or lumps that may have escaped earlier processes. The tobacco is now ready to be packed in bulk, though it is left yet another month for the aroma to reach its maximum. When thoroughly cured it is ready for making up into packets.

As a matter of curiosity an irregular method of curing tobacco may be described at this point. The leaves are taken in bundles of ten and dipped for fifteen minutes in a bath of tepid water containing nitrate of potassium. To give the tobacco an aroma a mixture is put in the aforesaid bath, made up as follows: a spoonful of coffee and honey or some similarly sweet substance, dissolved in alcohol and scented with two drops of essence of roses, one drop of sandalwood oil, and one of essence of wallflower. The stronger this compound the more will the tobacco resemble properly cured Virginia. When the leaves are sufficiently pliable they are rolled five together into the shape of "carrots" and placed in a tin-plate receptacle where they are kept for thirty-six hours. When fermentation has been completed the receptacle is opened and evaporation allowed to take place for a fortnight, the "carrots" being turned morning and evening. Then with scissors, razor blades or what not the tobacco can be shredded, dried and put on the market. Cigarette ends and tobacco substitutes are all of use in this fake tobacco; among the substitutes may be listed:

Flowers of magnolia, clover, lavender, elder and rose petals.

Leaves of walnut, ash, plane, chestnut, birch, pear, cherry, vine, fig, currant, rose, raspberry, bean, tomato, artichoke, carrot, beetroot, maize.

Wild plants such as wormwood, clover, verbena, centaury, arnica, balm, sage, marshmallow, burdock, borage.

The preparation of these substitutes is very simple. The leaves are moistened and the veins removed; the flowers or leaves are then left to soak for twenty-four hours in water containing a pinch of carbonate of potash, and then dried in the dark after having been cut small.

There were other plants which our forefathers enjoyed smoking, chief among which was coltsfoot—an excellent substitute for tobacco. The flower resembles the dandelion, and the plant grows in damp places among the fields and ditches. To prepare it for smoking the veins are removed from the leaves and before the latter get too dry they are soaked for two days in salt water. They are then cut up, put back in salt water for another couple of days, taken out and drained and then dried in the sun. Pliny recommended coltsfoot as we have already seen; we in turn prescribe it for asthma and bronchitis. It can also be used to eke out tobacco in the event of a shortage. During the Occupation great scope was

afforded to the ingenuity of the French smoker, and he found
coltsfoot invaluable. The fact is worth noting; one never knows!

The world consumption of tobacco is immense. In Great Britain
during the fifty years from 1900-49 the revenue from its sale rose
from £11,000,000 a year to £602,000,000. In other countries
the increase has been proportionate and it would be difficult to
assess the annual tonnage consumed. In order of quantity the
tobacco-producing countries are: India, U.S.A., Russia, Brazil,
Greece, Japan, Turkey, Italy, Bulgaria and France.

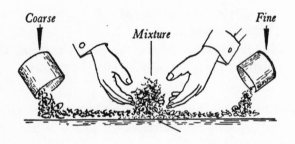

Coarse cut and fine cut tobacco can be mixed to the taste of the
smoker by a sweep of the wrist that comes with practice (see
above). The coarse cut makes a useful element in such a mixture;
it is more pliable than the fine cut and less cohesive. It is, indeed,
the better tobacco for packing a pipe bowl and it draws better; but
the two cuts go well together and make an admirable mixture.

Nicotine being very volatile, dry tobacco will be less charged
with it than moist. In consequence, even tobacco of the same brand
will have a varying taste according to whether it is fresh or dry.
It is for the smoker to choose which he prefers. Too fresh, the
aroma is not fully developed and the smoke is less pleasant to the
nostrils; the tobacco produces more moisture in the bowl, soon
fouls the pipe, and necessitates harder drawing; it tends not to

burn so evenly nor so well, being particularly hard on the interior of the bowl. If the tobacco be too dry the smoke is less smooth in the mouth, which it dries up, with a consequent irritation of the papillæ. It tends to burn too quickly, and this too rapid combustion being independent of the smoker, is contrary to the normal action of the pipe.

Needless to say, the advantages and disadvantages of either of these hygrometric conditions vary according to the materials concerned. Dry tobacco goes better in a clay pipe than in a briar; a corncob will give a good smoke from either; a virgin pipe that has never been smoked will give no satisfaction with either. Such examples might be multiplied. Every condition of the tobacco requires a different technique—looser packing in the bowl for moist, together with harder drawing; very short puffs for the dry; in a word, the most careful adapting of the smoker's action according to the nature of his pipe and the degree it has been seasoned.

It is only by personal experience that the smoker can gauge to a nicety his ideals with regard to the condition of his tobacco. For our own part we prefer it rather dry, having observed that in this state it yields the maximum of its bouquet, whereas moisture makes it niggardly in this respect. But all this is of really less importance than the quality of the pipe—it is upon the pipe that the satisfactory burning of the tobacco depends; everything else is more or less a corollary of that one requisite. It must never be forgotten whatever else we may do to ensure that luck be with us —we must never lose sight of the importance of the pipe.

THE TOBACCO JAR

The smoker who buys his ounce of tobacco as he requires it has no actual need of a tobacco jar; nevertheless, even in those circumstances we are not against its adoption, even by those who for one reason or another find themselves mobile. We are not against it because it possesses certain sovereign advantages. Tobacco in the jar keeps fresh while it matures, the jar playing much the same part in the maturing of tobacco as the barrel does in the keeping of wine—within it the tobacco decants itself and becomes perfect. Osmosis exists between the two—the material of the jar acts on the tobacco, and by moistening the latter some smokers are able to tell the nature of the jar in which it has been kept. This is indeed the domain of osmology.

Keeping tobacco in a jar will not prevent the smoker from getting a fill for his pipe, or from replenishing his pouch before going for a walk. Moreover, he will get a better smoke than if he just bought an ounce at the shop round the corner, without any notion of its hygrometric condition.

Before laying in their stock some smokers place at the bottom of the jar a sliced carrot or potato in order to keep it fresh; others put in a piece of orange peel as being more fragrant; yet others sprinkle a few drops of rum or brandy on the tobacco when the jar is full. There is nothing to be said against any of these practices, and the matter must be left entirely to the smoker to do as he sees fit. In tobacco, as in everything else, it is purely a matter of taste that must guide us; it is for the smoker to obtain the maximum of pleasure from his tobacco, and the tobacco jar will not fail to aid him in this quest.

Tobacco jars are to be found made of the most diverse—and even of the most rare—materials, some of which are admirably suited for the purpose; they range from sandstone to the delicate wood of the lemon tree, and can be of iron, tin, silver, ivory, glass, horn, boxwood, birch, mahogany, cherrywood, etc. It is difficult to choose any one in preference to another, but it may be taken as a rule that the simplest and most convenient, such as the stone jar, are the best. Many smokers use an old grease pot which they fill with tobacco and seal hermetically, the aroma and quality of the mixture demanding that the receptacle should be airtight.

The most useful purpose of the tobacco jar is to preserve the contents from deterioration. Tobacco is very sensitive not only to variations in temperature but also to the slightest changes in its surroundings; it even absorbs the odor of anything in its vicinity. According to the neighborhood in which the smoker lives, so must he take the appropriate measures. A stone jar has the advantage of being capacious and very strong. There is no mistake about it, it knows how to conserve and improve what is entrusted to its care!

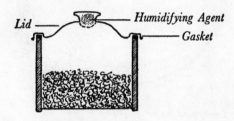

One might amuse oneself profitably by concocting mixtures of tobacco from any of the brands upon the market, though any reputable tobacconist will save the smoker the trouble by making up and keeping by him the recipe of any mixture to his liking. We once made a marvelous blend of coarse and fine cut with a touch of perique; this was packed in a stone jar and sealed hermetically by placing a rag soaked in rum under the lid and closing down the whole by a strong elastic band, as illustrated on page 82. It was left for an entire college term, not to be opened until the vacation. The great occasion was a wet summer's day; the memory of that glorious moment lingers yet, a symbol of what may be attained—it was what the pipe had been waiting for since the day of its making. It is in that light that we can look upon the tobacco jar—as a prelude to filling one's pipe, a preliminary to a perfect smoke. What the jar exhales is but a promise of what the pipe will fulfill.

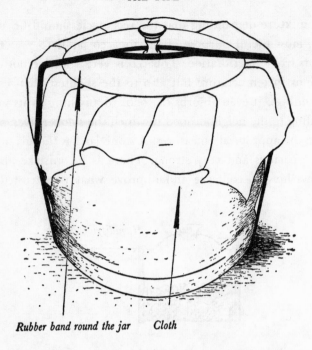

Rubber band round the jar   *Cloth*

THE SNUFFBOX

The custom of taking tobacco through the nose in the form of snuff is of purely European origin. It was used, as an aperitif is taken nowadays, on the pretext of sharpening the appetite. Snuff has been taken for headaches and for toothache. It was formerly as much a matter of fashion and routine as smoking a cigarette is now; it gave a man self-confidence. In both cases the spirit of the age is reflected.

Among the more celebrated snuff-takers were several Popes, though in this context mention should be made of Urban VIII and Innocent XI who prohibited taking snuff in church on account of the disturbance created by the continual snapping open and shut of the snuffboxes. Louis XIV and Louis XV were snuff-takers; so were such great figures as Napoleon, Frederick the Great, Voltaire, Talleyrand, Rousseau, etc. A glance at the ledgers of the famous house of Fribourg and Treyer, of London, reveals that in Britain royalty, nobility and the middle classes were all great snuff-takers.

Snuff was originally sold in solid "carrots" which the purchaser had to grind up for his own use in a little pocket mill or grater, and it was this among other things that inspired the campaign against the noisy and offensive habit of taking it. Not only was it forbidden, as we have seen, in church, but priests who had fallen victim to the "inveterate vice" were obliged to abstain from it for at least an hour before and two hours after saying Mass. A synodal ordinance of 1698 lays it down that, "We forbid all ecclesiastics to indulge in the custom of taking tobacco in powder form, particularly and without exception in church, so that this scandalous indecency in the very House of God should be finally done away with."

The snuffbox played a considerable part in diplomatic relations during the seventeenth and eighteenth centuries. A man's breeding was judged by his manner with the snuffbox. In addition to its proper function of containing powdered tobacco, it was used to carry a portrait or some other delicate miniature on or inside the lid. It was the wrist watch of the period, but much more picturesque and artistic. The art of the jeweler was enlisted to enrich it with diamonds and precious stones. One of the finest specimens belonged to the Duc de Lauzun; it was adorned with a portrait of Mademoiselle de Montpensier, the King's mistress, and Lauzun had the temerity to show it to Louis XIV himself. It was Louis' physician Fagon, by the way, who once sent an assistant named Barbin to deliver to the Académie Française a discourse that he (Fagon) had composed against the practice of using tobacco. All the time he was reading it Barbin never ceased from taking pinch after pinch of snuff, to such a degree that the audience was in fits of laughter and the whole diatribe fizzled out. Fagon was himself a snuff addict, though he indulged in private. That evening the King lost no opportunity of laughing at his physician who, enraged beyond measure, dismissed his assistant with ignominy.

The diplomatic status of the snuffbox—used by sovereigns as a medium for exchanging portraits—attained its greatest height toward the end of the eighteenth century, after which it appeared less often among the wedding gifts of noble brides (Marie Antoinette received more than fifty when she went to France). It changed in appearance too, pretty pictures giving place to designs and patterns; in Revolutionary France there were even snuffboxes ornamented with a guillotine! The Terror passed, and under the Consulate the guillotine was replaced by the weeping willow. Napoleon's set-back with the Persian Ambassador (see page 5) put him against smoking, but he was a prodigious snuffer.* Innumerable snuffboxes passed through his hands, but they were either dashed to the ground in one of his outbursts of temper or were given to those about him when he was in a genial mood. At the time of his downfall, the Emperor's little three-cornered hat had become so popular that snuffboxes were made to resemble it, and though proscribed by the authorities, the shape was a favorite throughout the Restoration and for long afterward. Nor should the fact be overlooked by Frenchmen today that, when the representatives of the Great Powers were gathered round the table at the Congress of Vienna, Talleyrand circulated his elegant snuffbox with its equally choice contents and won for France her former frontiers and a seat in the councils of Europe.

Snuff-taking having largely given place to smoking, the snuffbox was replaced by the tobacco jar, but despite the difference in size

---

* As the Emperor was too impatient to pull out of his pocket a snuffbox, open it, take a pinch, close it and replace it in his pocket, he had a leather-lined pocket sewn into his waistcoat and carried his snuff loose in it. Frederick the Great had a similar pocket in his coat.

and shape the functions of both remain the same—to keep the tobacco in good condition.

THE POUCH

The smoker who has no receptacle for tobacco but his jar will be
limited in the scene of his smoking to the house, unless he carries
a loose supply of tobacco in his pocket. This is not recommended,
though on desperate occasions desperate measures must be adopted
and the shreds and loose bits in a pocket may be scraped together
to get that last pipe. At the bottom of the pocket are to be found
fluff and other imponderable, indefinable substances that are liable
to spoil tobacco, hinder its burning and ruin its taste.

A sensible and convenient way of getting over this difficulty is
to carry a tobacco pouch. This is a sort of pocket sack, and may
range from an old sock to a leather bag closed with a zipper.
Rubber and leather are the principal materials employed for
pouches, and they can be divided into those two categories.

LEATHER.   A primitive form of pouch consists simply of a piece
of leather cut in the round and gathered together by a cord. When
the string is drawn the bag closes to form a pocket to hold the
tobacco. The pouch hangs from the belt like an old-fashioned
purse.

This pattern has been improved upon in the course of generations. The most common pouch now in use is made from a
rectangle of leather doubled over lengthwise and sewn along the
edges. At the top of one side an opening is made the whole
length, which is closed with a zipper or some similar device. This
design of pouch has been yet more improved by the addition of a
lining of cellophane or some other waterproof and airtight material which will seal the pouch when it is closed.

These two patterns indicate the career of the leather tobacco pouch through the course of the ages. Among other practical devices mention may be made of the box containing leather bellows and closing automatically. Another type took the form of a small handbag with a device for closing it. Even if these pouches were less practical they offered as many advantages as our modern ones, and many were in common use until they disappeared from the market.

RUBBER.   A very ingenious and useful form of rubber pouch, found more often on the Continent than in Britain or the United States, is illustrated on this page. It consists of a circular rubber bag the opening of which has been made with a twist in it so that when not in use the bag is closed. To open it one need only pull the edge of the bag and it untwists, ready for the pipe to be filled. A pouch with a flap is less airtight than the preceding but longer-lived and in some ways more handy.

Yet another type of pouch, which may be made of rubber or of very pliable leather, consists of the usual bag or pocket, with one side prolonged to a considerable length so that the pocket may be rolled round and round in it. A pouch such as this may be made of silk or some other material so long as the actual tobacco container is lined with fine rubber, cellophane, pig's bladder or what is known technically as skive. It is even possible to make a pouch from the inner tube of a car tire!

Open

Flap

Closed

SELECTION OF A POUCH.   A good tobacco pouch should possess the following qualities:

1. It should allow the smoker to fill his pipe easily without the loss of a single shred of tobacco; which means that it should be large enough for him to insert the bowl of his pipe held in the thumb and forefinger of his left hand while the right is comfortably employed in packing it.

2. It must keep the tobacco fresh for a long time.

3. It must keep it free of any foreign substances that might injure it.

Leather pouches fulfill the first of these desiderata; rubber pouches are best for the last two.

A pocket tobacco box—whether of metal or other material—is not recommended, for the tobacco is apt to break and crumble into dust, which does not occur in a pouch on account of its pliability. A pouch, moreover, is no more inconvenient to carry than a pocketbook, and when flat it goes easily into a breast or side pocket even when it holds a couple of ounces of tobacco.

A confirmed smoker will not spend longer than he need on the question of a pouch. If he empties it in twenty-four or even forty-eight hours he will have started by filling his pipe with fresh tobacco and ended by smoking dust—in other words he will have run through the exquisite gamut from fresh to extra dry. His pipe will thus have afforded him infinite variety, apart from any question of whether it was made of wood or other material.

It is, it should be said, possible to develop a technique whereby tobacco may be kept in its original paper packet without using a pouch at all. This calls for a certain dexterity in opening the packet, and it must be closed tightly each time after use. It is not the ideal procedure, but it does quite well for anyone who smokes his ounce or more in less than forty-eight hours. Obviously the air must be excluded and the packet is best kept in a trouser pocket on account of the wearer's natural warmth (excellent for tobacco). It is a good plan to keep the packet closed with a rubber band.

Some few tobaccos are actually packaged in the form of a small, roll-up type of pouch, and this is, of course, ideal for the smoker who doesn't want to bother transferring his tobacco to a pouch. Let us hope he likes the brand of tobacco which he buys for the sake of convenience.

GENERALITIES.   There are two sorts of pipe smokers: those who smoke a pipe only; and those who vary it with an occasional cigarette. Needless to say, the cigarette smoker who occasionally smokes a pipe comes under neither of these categories. The hygrometric condition of tobacco is a matter of little concern to the last mentioned unless he is in the habit of making his own cigarettes; but it is important to the first two sorts of smokers, and it is to their benefit that our remarks are addressed.

If the tobacco is too moist it may be exposed for a moment to the heat of a fire or the warmth of the sun, but it is best to do so in the shade either in the open air, if it is a fine day, or in a dry place. It is never good to expose tobacco directly to the sun's rays; the changes of temperature are too sudden, drawing out the aroma and leaving only the smell of hay.

If it is too dry—as inevitably happens in hot or dry climates —a hermetically-sealed tobacco jar becomes practically indispensable. Take an empty stoneware jam jar with a rubber-ring top or lid, empty into it the contents of the packet and sprinkle a little water over it all; then, having sealed the jar, expose it to the heat of the fire or to the sun's rays. In less than an hour the tobacco will be as perfect as may be desired. Clearly it is only worth while to do this with a reasonable quantity of tobacco. A good pipe is no use without good tobacco, and tobacco is not good unless it is in proper hygrometric condition.

It should be observed that in windy localities fresh tobacco is essential for a pipe that has no lid, otherwise the wind blows away the contents of the bowl instantly. Fresh tobacco stays in the pipe better than dry, and the smoker who prefers the latter must take suitable steps and get himself a pipe with a lid.

In Morocco—as formerly in China and the adjacent countries— pipe and tobacco are carried in a leather bag hung around the neck, called by the Moors a "beite." Like some modern pouches, this bag contains several pockets, one for the tobacco, another for the pipe, a third for flint, steel and tinder to light it. The smoker opens his "beite," takes a pinch of tobacco in the hollow of his hand and presses it into the "adham" (see illustration, page 31). He then takes a piece of flint and some tinder between the thumb and forefinger of his left hand, strikes a spark and lights the tinder, which he pushes into the bowl. When the tobacco is burning he gives one pull at his pipe and then passes it on to his friends. Every country has its customs. We no longer do as the Moors, but we should never forget that Nature always helps us to supply our needs, even when they are of our own making.

THE PIPE RACK

The pipe rack is an object of great importance from both a moral and a utilitarian point of view.

It is commonly made of a strip of wood about a foot or eighteen inches long and two and a half inches wide, in which a number of slots are cut, as illustrated here, which are to hold the

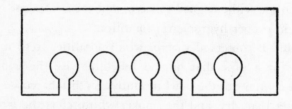

stems of the pipes. This strip can be fixed to the wall in a variety of ways, being either attached at right angles to another piece of wood nailed to the wall, or hung on screw-eyes, or secured by metal or wooden brackets.

It would be difficult to assert that this kind of rack is the best; there are many other types that are more practical, more finished and more ornamental; it is here described as the simplest. If this type of rack be decided upon it is essential to see that it is absolutely at right angles to the wall in order to ensure that the pipes do not fall out of their slots; it is better for it to be tilted upward than downward, as shown on page 91. Anything else—appearance or whatnot—is of purely secondary importance to this.

MATERIAL ADVANTAGES OF A RACK.

Even as the horizontal is the proper position for a pipe when being smoked, so is the upright position proper for it when at rest.*

Some captious souls may contend that this depends upon circumstances. One can, indeed, buy so-called "pipe holders" in which the mouthpiece is held uppermost. We pass these by without comment, leaving such stupidity to expose itself.

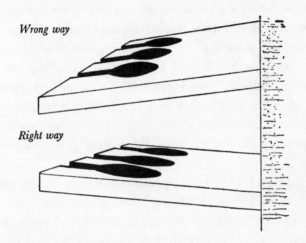

It is useless to deny that the proper position prescribed above presents certain inconveniences, particularly if the smoker fails to practice the precepts we shall lay down with regard to cleaning his pipe (page 125). But they are inconveniences for which he will have only himself to blame. This is especially the case when, after a smoke, the pipe is laid down on a table or some such horizontal object and the nicotine allowed to soak into the grain of the already heated wood, no trouble having been taken to pass a pipe cleaner through the mouthpiece and stem.

* By this we mean with the bowl uppermost—that being to a pipe what his head is to a man—the capital (*caput*, head)—part.

This stagnation of the nicotine in one of the most vital parts of the pipe causes harm such as the owners of "pipe holders" can scarcely have envisaged. The harm can, however, be averted if, as soon as the pipe has been smoked, it is restored to its perpendicular position—always supposing the smoker has exercised the usual care demanded of him. If the pipe is put in the rack without being cleaned the nicotine liberated while smoking drains down inside the stem and collects into a drop at the mouthpiece. When the smoker takes up his pipe again, the warmth of his lips will loosen this drop and he will draw into his mouth enough nicotine to ruin the smoke and make him drop the pipe, spluttering with the foul taste in his mouth. He will be forced to rinse out his mouth thoroughly and will have to clean the pipe no less thoroughly. Even after rinsing his mouth he will learn to his cost, by repeated expectoration, how long it takes for the gustatory papillæ to recover and free themselves from the violent compounds of nicotine.

The pipe rack is an ideal apparatus not only for the calm and methodical smoker but also, and more particularly, for the careless smoker, for it will force him, if he wants to enjoy his pipe, to keep it in a perfectly clean condition—a habit that may make him impatient at the outset but to which he will submit willingly when he perceives the excellent results that ensue.

There can be little purpose in reinforcing the prejudices of those who look with repugnance upon a pipe and with, perhaps, even greater repugnance upon its smoker, so we may as well seize this opportunity to liquidate the difficult matter of spitting.

A pipe does not make one spit except occasionally when it is lighted and then it is mainly at the choice of the smoker, and even a habit he may contract. In any event, it causes spitting no more than does a cigarette. The man who spits when he pulls at his pipe is no real smoker. The good smoker does not spit, save for that initial and fundamental expectoration which he may indulge in.

Spitting must be the outcome of some organic defect in the spitter; as is well known, the pipe smoker enjoys a perfect digestive constitution. And suppose he does spit! If analyzed, his sputum would be found less noxious than that of the drawing-room tea drinker.

MORAL ADVANTAGES OF THE PIPE RACK.   There can be no doubt that it is more attractive to look at pipes in a rack than to see them jumbled in a box. One of the inconveniences of this latter state of confusion is that the smoker has to examine each separately when choosing one to smoke. The pipes are not ranged in rank before the eye as in a rack where a single glance suffices to pick out the one wanted.

The given moment calls for its particular pipe. With a box this quick selection is not possible, even when every pipe answers to its name. Naturally the question does not arise when the smoker has no more than a mere half-dozen pipes, but for others it is important. There is a psychological moment when the exactly proper pipe in the rack presents itself for smoking, but if it be in a box one has to rummage about, always with the risk that one of its companions, less suitable for the moment, however excellent it may be in itself, may be taken after all.

No such mistake can be made with a pipe rack. On going off to work or for pleasure there is need only to cast one's eye over the panoply of fifty pipes or so in the racks to pick instantly on the one, the one and only pipe, with its mute and inexplicable appeal, its cry that it wants to be smoked.

It may be objected that these remarks apply to briar pipes rather than to meerschaum, porcelain and other more fragile kinds. That depends on the smoker's character, his way of life, the state of his nerves and those of his relatives. A pipe-box for fragile pipes is all right so long as one handles the contents with care, especially when the pipes have the stem of a piece with the bowl, as in the case of clay. But the question of choice is no less weighty.

For our part, we have resolved the problem of clay pipes—in a manner that seems absolutely conclusive—by using screw-eyes plugged into the wall as we have below. The ring supports the pipe by the bowl and averts any possibility of its being knocked or jerked out of the slot of a pipe rack. To ensure greater security a smaller screw-eye can be plugged in lower down to hold the stem. These screw-eyes are useful for holding smaller pipes, and it is worth nothing that they can be screwed into a board to keep the pipes safe in the event of moving house.

Needless to say, the smoker can modify or improve any of these methods as seems good to him; the important thing is to have one's

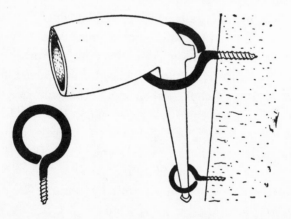

whole battery of pipes under one's eye. Even from the decorative point of view it is better to look at a panoply of pipes than at some so-called "artistic" daub hanging on the wall. Apart from the taste that is peculiar to it, each pipe is associated with its own memories. It is pleasant to enjoy one pipe after another; this one, maybe, recalling some happy event in one's life, that other bringing to mind the person who gave it, yet a third renewing by its smell the memory of a particular place or one particular day. As you smoke you will contemplate your collection of pipes that by their very existence grow ever more precious and cherished. From its place in the rack each pipe speaks as does a book from the shelf. Its eager words may be heard and understood only by those who, after much practice, have attuned their ears and their hearts. A pipe can be enjoyed without so much as its being lit.

CONCLUSIONS. If the truth be told, we ourselves make little use of pipe rack or box; we are content to hang our pipes on nails in the wall. If the nail be long enough and driven in far enough, slanting upward, the rim of the bowl will rest against the surface of the wall and keep the pipe steady (see below). This method must not be taken as a model, however. A simple nail will not hold a new pipe so well while the interior of the bowl retains its polish. But as soon as a pipe begins to char the nail will be quite sufficient, for it will catch better. There are, however, some shapes of bowl such as that shown below that clearly do not lend themselves to this method of hanging—or acrobatics, as one might say. Pipes of this shape should either be kept in some other way or hung on a nail driven in at a much sharper angle.

It is clear that the simple pipe rack can be adopted in a variety of designs and alternatives. None of them is perfect, though some attain a near perfection. A tobacco jar may be devoted to this purpose to considerable advantage, and if it be big enough it will

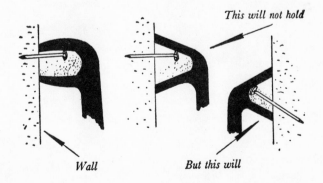

This will not hold

Wall   *But this will*

hold a number of pipes of all sorts and sizes. Even the sheath in which the mower carries the whetstone for his scythe can be adapted; or a shell case from the battlefield. There is, indeed, no limit to the choice of suitable pipe racks.

Part Three

FILLING THE PIPE

Having passed in review whatever concerns the pipe, we now find ourselves faced with three definite and concrete matters: the pipe we have chosen, a packet of tobacco, and the flame that is to serve as a liaison officer to bring these two essential factors into communication one with the other. We are to see how the contents should be packed in the container, how it should be lighted and then smoked with the maximum of delight to the gustatory-olfactory nerves.

As this book is written as much for amateurs as for professional smokers, for novices as for hardened practitioners, it has been thought best to suppose ourselves furnished with a briar pipe that has already been smoked. Instructions on seasoning the pipe will be given later.

It must not be imagined that tobacco can be rammed no matter how into the bowl of a pipe, that it is a matter of no importance how it is done, that a pipe can be treated as cavalierly as a cigarette. The gravest mishaps are likely to occur from the outset if this view is taken. There may be difficulties in drawing, the pipe may burn down at one side; it will certainly put up a self-defense impossible to foresee. The man who fills his pipe as he would the kitchen stove is treating it as no better than a cigarette and will certainly be paid back in his own coin.

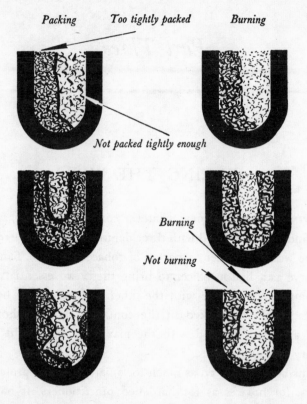

From the illustration above we get some notion of what happens when the pipe is filled in this slapdash fashion; particular notice should be paid to the effect of partial combustion. In such conditions it follows naturally that the effluvium is lost and the pipe itself ruined.

What is the proper way to fill a pipe?

In the first place, and above all else, fill it in pinches of tobacco.

The first pinch from the pouch, jar or packet should be just laid at the bottom of the bowl; which means that only a small

First Pinch   *Second Pinch*

quantity should be taken, for it will be the lowest portion of the
dottle. A good smoker will insert his finger to feel that all is right
before going any further. The subsequent pinches should be
gradually and more consistently laid, with an increasing pressure
of the forefinger as the top of the bowl is reached. This action
should be as mechanical as that of blowing through the mouthpiece before starting to fill, in order to make sure that the stem
is clear, or of glancing into the bowl and tapping it against the
palm of the hand, much as one would pat a horse about to run in
a race.

When the bowl is full to the brim a final pressure should be
given by the thumb—an action calling for a subtle artistry that
can be acquired only by use. This thumb pressure suppresses any
possible unevenness in the lighting surface of the tobacco and
gives a finishing touch to the filling. It is essential that the surface
of the packed tobacco should be perfectly even in order to facilitate the operation of lighting.

All this being done, the next thing is to draw on the pipe to
discover what resistance the tobacco in the bowl offers to the
passage of air. If it flows too freely, another pressure of the
thumb is called for and another pinch of tobacco must be put in

*Press final
lighting
surface
with thumb*

Third Pinch

the bowl; this latter is not, however, essential but it is recommended to facilitate lighting. It is a more serious matter if the drawing is too difficult; there is then practically nothing to be done but to empty the bowl completely and start filling all over again. It may be that a shred of tobacco is blocking the opening from the bowl into the stem. In that event it must be pushed out with a pipe cleaner or some similarly adequate object. A good smoker will see at a glance what is the reason for his pipe drawing badly; though with him such incidents will occur but seldom, for even as he fills his pipe he will keep on drawing at it to see if the packing should be looser or firmer. If there is a blockage at the first pinch, there is clearly a shred in the passage and it will be necessary to unpack the bowl. Having put things right the smoker will repack his pipe, put it between his teeth, administer the terminal and fundamental thumb pressure, and light up.

An inexperienced smoker may well be disgusted with his pipe after several bad fillings, but the blame is solely his own. A pipe properly and firmly packed gives better smoking than one lightly packed; but that again is a matter of individual preference. In any event it is necessary before all else that the technique here described should be followed, from the first pinch of tobacco to the final pressure of the thumb.

The beginner must now be enlightened on the subject of aeration. Coarse cut tobacco makes an easier filling than fine cut; the successive pinches can be inserted with little risk of a serious blockage. Experience also proves that it is easier to pack with dry

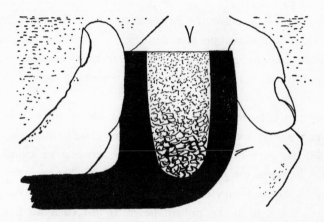

tobacco than with fresh. The former offers a certain elasticity which the other lacks. With dry tobacco, if it is packed down firmly, the filling has a tendency to spring up again to its original level; with fresh, it will lie flat and tight against the walls of the bowl, making a sort of compact wad that sooner or later has got to be aerated. It was for this reason that such stress was laid on filling by pinches, no matter what the condition of the tobacco.

The most deplorable—and, alas, the most usual—way of filling a pipe is to put it in the pouch, holding it between the first and second fingers while the thumb rams in the tobacco as vigorously as though it were sawing a log or puttying up a leak. This method of procedure is more common with a tobacco jar than with a pouch. To those who retort that the taste of the tobacco is the same in any case, there is no answer save the dignified silence of the gourmet or the wine connoisseur.

Packing is an essential operation upon the proper conduct of which depends in great part the action of combustion. A badly packed pipe will make the novice feel poorly and induce in him a fatally false comparison between wood and paper, between the pipe and the cigarette. So he will hasten back to what is easier to smoke, and will never know the infinite variety of pleasure that can be procured from even one brand of tobacco when smoked in a selection of pipes, or the happiness to be had from different blends smoked in just one pipe only. He will prefer the monotonous sameness of the many brands of cigars and cigarettes—faced with the alternatives of satisfaction and poisoning he will choose the latter.

Perseverance is demanded, even of the old smoker, when he starts on his first simple briar. But nothing will discourage the man who has once realized the difference between an aroma and perfume, between the natural and the artificial, between the pipe and the cigarette. If, for example, for some reason the tobacco is too dry when put in the pouch, he must not turn up his nose at it but should know how to make good use of it. If he were to fill the pipe with this dry stuff, the probability is that he would get a good bit of it on his tongue at the first draw. The experienced smoker will make no such mistake; he will mix his dry tobacco with fresh. But supposing he has none of the latter handy? Then by shaking his pouch he will bring some coarser shreds to the top and these he will collect into a small pinch that he will place at the bottom of the bowl (see page 100). The remainder of the dust will go on top. In this way the pipe will be smokable, and he will have proved that proper packing can be effected no matter what the condition of the tobacco.

LIGHTING THE PIPE

HISTORICAL. FLINT AND STEEL.   The history of fire itself can never be written, but in these pages we are interested in the means employed to make it. Flint and steel have existed from the day man first discovered how to make fire at will. There was a moment when some man first struck a spark from a flint and set fire to a few dry twigs or leaves. From that day to this the method of fire-making has changed but little. In Corsica and elsewhere the peasants still obtain a spark by striking the tip of the knife against a flint, setting light to some form of tinder that takes the place of the original dry twigs.

There are two sorts of flint and steel lighters:

The Tinder Lighter. The lighter shown on page 104 consists in essence of a flint, a steel milled wheel, and a tinder wick.* By turning the wheel against the flint with a sharp flick, a spark is struck which sets light to the tinder. This tinder does not burst into flame, it merely smolders, and that is why this particular type of lighter is better for cigarettes than for pipes. It is safer, however, than the fluid lighter and with a little patience can be used with a pipe perfectly well. In wartime and other periods of difficulty it affords the maximum of security and efficiency.

The Fluid Lighter, shown on page 105, works on the same principle as the foregoing, except that the wick is finer and only breaks into flame when impregnated with a fluid like gasoline. This wick does not smolder, and in that lies its chief difference

---

* The tinder employed in these lighters is sometimes called "amadou," which the dictionary defines as "tinder prepared from a dried fungus steeped in saltpeter, used as a match or styptic."

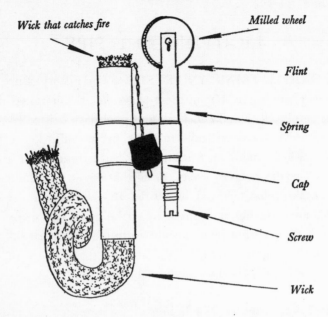

Wick that catches fire

Milled wheel

Flint

Spring

Cap

Screw

Wick

from the other. The modern lighter, with an automatic lid, is a
slight improvement upon its parent, but it is more a luxury than
a necessity, and of greater use to the cigarette smoker than to the
pipe m..n. The only real advantage it possesses lies in the lid
which, upon being opened, automatically strikes a spark that
may—or may not—light the wick. Despite the claims of the various
makers, there is no certainty that this lighter will invariably
function; it sometimes misfires, as does the old-fashioned flint
and steel about which no eulogies are sung.

Science is perfect only theoretically; it serves us but we have
to serve it. Fashion has brought the automatic lighter to the fore-
front, but its chief advantage, as we have observed, is that it
obviates the thumbwork on the wheel that was required by the
older type. This advantage is so slight, however, that we should
hesitate to recommend the fluid lighter above the many other
means of lighting a pipe.

To be fair, however, there is one excellent type of thumbwork

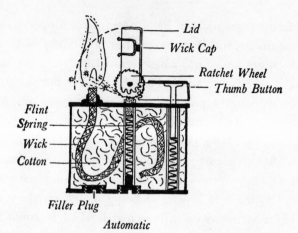

Automatic

on the wheel lighter which has the inestimable advantage of staying alight in a strong wind. The flame even improves in a wind, as soldiers and woodsmen will testify.

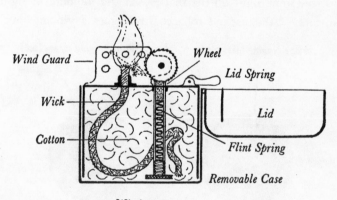

Windproof

The Match is a wooden firebrand, and is thus as old as the flint and steel. The only actual difference between them is one of cause and effect:

        2. *Flint.*

1. Fire.   3. Twig.   4. The firebrand or match.

        2. *Iron or steel.*

In the Middle Ages sticks of hemp were used, dipped in sulphur. It was not until 1805 that the sulphur was coated with chlorate of potash, sugar and gum, which ignited on touching sulphuric acid soaked in asbestos fiber. The old Lucifer match was a stick dipped in chlorate of potash paste with antimony sulphide and ignited by friction on sandpaper. Congreves were an improvement on these, and by 1830 a portable match was in production. It was not until 1855 that amorphous phosphorus was invented and the match as we know it came into being, the lighting material being transferred to the box instead of being placed on the tip of the match. There are many varieties of match which it would be fruitless to enumerate.

HOW TO LIGHT UP. Some experienced pipe smokers recognize two—if not three—ways of lighting a pipe, and our diagrams may throw some light on the matter. At the moment of lighting, the surface of the packed tobacco undergoes a violent shock or

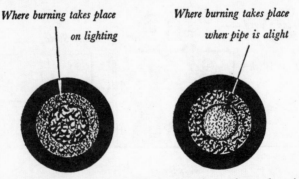

Where burning takes place on lighting

Where burning takes place when pipe is alight

convulsion that tends to upset the operation of combustion (see illustration). The particles turn red hot, brown, or glowing, and curl up in a confused way so that the smoker cannot tell at first whether or not the fire has reached the whole wall of the bowl. It will, therefore, be necessary to take an ashtray, saucer, envelope or some other object with a flat surface (a box of matches will do) and place it over the bowl as soon as the tobacco is alight,

Ember   *Match*

carefully smooth the burning particles into place, strike another match and once again—this time definitely—light the tobacco. This is the simplest and most rational way of ensuring even combustion in a properly filled pipe.

There is, however, another method, almost as good and more speedy, shown above, which consists in pressing a piece of crumpled paper over the bowl, making a cap of it, and applying the lighted match to the center, at the same time drawing in gently but rapidly. It is rarely that the tobacco does not light evenly. This method also works excellently with an ember from the fire placed in the center as before. In either case the paper must be such as burns easily, and not too thin. A spent match can be lighted by this means, as illustrated.

We have no preference for either of these devices, but we are most emphatically on the side of smokers who spread the burning evenly, and against those who let the lighting of a pipe take care of itself; better burn one's thumb than leave things to chance.

The even lighting of a pipe makes for easy drawing as it ensures, so to speak, a good start-off for smoking. The advantage of having an even burning surface, when smoking in the open air, is shown in the illustration on page 108, which shows the wind blowing away the burning tobacco, leaving an empty bowl, whereas an even surface presents nothing for the breeze to catch.

This method of filling a pipe is fortified to a remarkable ex-

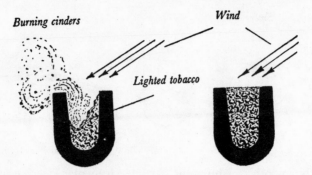

tent by every smoker's experience. Yet the careless smoker who neglects to level the burning surface or even to press his thumb on the final packing, will even leave the tobacco hanging over the rim of the bowl, reckoning that the shreds will be burned when the pipe is alight. Others, in a greater hurry, have the habit of turning the pipe to one side or the other, as illustrated below, to make the flame catch the tobacco. There is no sense whatever in doing this for the flame is drawn down by the suction of the smoker and can be directed to every part of the top of the bowl, as we see in the companion illustration. Indeed, such senseless treatment of a pipe is proof of sheer, culpable negligence. Other smokers go so far as to turn their pipe upside down under the impression that it will light better. Apart from the fact that materials such as meerschaum recover from such treat-

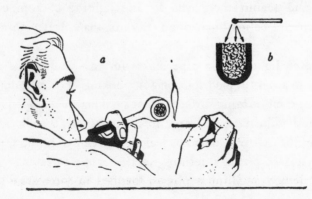

ment with difficulty, it is highly inconvenient not to be able to tell where the flame has caught the tobacco. Things such as the foregoing should never be done except under the stress of circumstances. The object is to obtain a satisfactory light for one's pipe; and to do this it is best to utilize the phenomenon of the returning flame which occurs between the mouth of the smoker and the bowl of his pipe when he lights the tobacco—a phenomenon provoked by a series of short and regular inhalations familiar to all experienced smokers—who have often burned their eyebrows!

WHAT SHALL WE USE? It is no matter what the pipe is lit with so long as the lighter liberates no noxious fumes that may (a) spoil the effluence of the smoke in injecting malodorous particles that cling to the tobacco, and (b) affect unfavorably the receptivity of the mouth.

Elements such as these must therefore be avoided, and among the worst may be mentioned the flame of a gas lighter, a sulphur match, and the wax taper.

An ordinary wood or Swedish match is on all accounts the best of these artificial lighters, but an ember from a wood fire deserves a whole paragraph to itself. It is the queen of all lighters, and any smoker who cares to make the experiment will speedily recognize its superiority over any other method of lighting a pipe. The pipe lit with such an ember—especially if it be of some resinous wood—will afford thirty per cent more pleasure and satisfaction than if a match or fluid lighter be used. This admits of no question, experience alone will convince the skeptic; it has to be tried to bring full convincement. Imagine coming into camp after a long day's tramp; dark has fallen and the log fire is blazing clearly and merrily; and then to be nourished—no other word will do—by a great pipe lit by a smoldering stick from the fire! It is at such times that all theories hatched when smok-

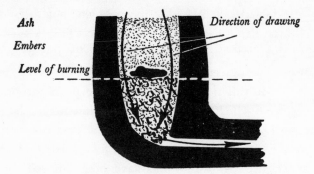

Ash

Embers

Level of burning

Direction of drawing

ing in one's study go by the board, when the whiff of the pipe mingles with the robust, health-giving smell of a wood fire.

It should be understood, naturally, that the glowing ember placed on the surface of the tobacco must be left among the burning shreds until the pipe is properly alight. We would even go so far as to advise pressing it in with the thumb, for not only will it communicate its perfume to the tobacco, but even when burned out it will assist drawing, merely by its presence in the bowl (see the drawing above). It is impossible to overrate its virtues.

The pipe with a lid has the advantage of retaining the burning tobacco without the need to have recourse to any other expedient; in its way it takes the place of the thumb or the matchbox pressed on the bowl. Pipe lids are on sale that can be fitted to

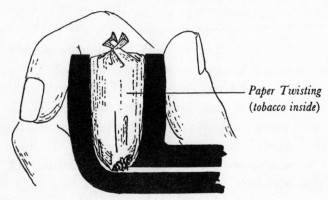

*Paper Twisting
(tobacco inside)*

almost any bowl. But nothing takes the place of the pressure of the thumb—it is alive and not inert, as the end of a pencil, nor limited to the surface of the bowl, as a matchbox.

It is even possible to buy fills of tobacco packed in wisps of thin paper and ready to insert in the bowl of a pipe. Whatever the conveniences of this sort of thing, illustrated on page 110, it seems as useless a contrivance as it is harmful on account of the putting tobacco into the bowl. There is, however, need to mention it in a book on smoking, although the practice is slowly dying out.

COMBUSTION

We have now reached the climax of this treatise. All the requisite conditions have been fulfilled; nothing now remains but to carry the enterprise of smoking through to the very last whiff. But before coming to practical points let us indulge in a little theory.

PRELIMINARIES.   Let us start by laying it down that when one smokes one does not blow out the cheeks, as simple folk seem to think or as some foolish advertisements would make us believe; on the contrary, in smoking one draws in the cheeks. To puff them out would be to blow down the stem in order to fan the burning tobacco, but apart from the fact that it would be a useless effort—for a pipe cannot be forced, it draws as it sees fit—such procedure would have little effect on the normal process of combustion. It might, indeed, ensure that the tobacco was burning right round the wall of the bowl, but it is not a thing that can be recommended. Smoking is more a matter for the lips than for the cheeks.

Smoke is a mixture of gas, steam and some more or less tenuous particles that are set free in the course of combustion; the smoke from the bowl is blue as it rises; after passing through the stem and mouthpiece it turns yellow; if one blows into the pipe through the mouthpiece yellow and blue smoke arise at the same time from the bowl. These colors are more or less relative, and much of the smoke appears gray. This smoke is pleasant to look at, and that is why there is so little pleasure in smoking in the dark. The sight of the smoke plays a considerable part in helping one to direct the combustion or rather educe it; without seeing it one loses control. But it is principally the odorous particles contained in the smoke that are of interest, and it is for that reason that the smoke should be charged with them as fully as possible, which is where the smoker comes in.

The cigarette symbolizes perfume; the pipe has a monopoly of odor. Whereas the latter is the product of Nature, the former is the product of man. Pierre Louys calls the cigarette the spiral phantom of Greek beauty, the sole new form of voluptuousness devised since the days of antiquity.

COMBUSTION PROPER.   All the conditions so far laid down having been observed does not necessarily mean that the smoking of a pipe can be satisfactorily achieved without the observance of yet more rules. Smoking is no spontaneous action; combustion is not accomplished of itself, its realization can be born only of a clear conscience.

When you smoke—or maybe when you used to smoke—a cigarette there is the inclination to prolong the pleasure, to savor it (Latin *sapor*, a taste). It is tossed away only when the end becomes too charged with nicotine and is disagreeable to the mouth and nostrils. It is not the same with a pipe. Where the cigarette finishes with a nasty fag-end, the pipe produces a dottle which it is not only a pleasure but a duty to smoke. A cigarette smoked badly and thus spoiled is no great loss. Not so with a pipe. In the cigarette the tobacco container burns at the same time as its contents; with a pipe the container remains, and smoking too quickly or carelessly will damage it. In the cigarette the container is a temporary tube, to be thrown away—what is left of it—when too foul to smoke; in the pipe this tube matures and seasons, preparing itself to yield an ever-increasing excellence in future smokes. So this precious instrument must not be spoiled, it must be maintained in good condition; what is more, it must be perfected and nurtured, lubricated and fashioned.

Smoking should be a rite—perhaps not a ceremony but at least an act of self-communion and contemplation.

The deliberate frequency, what may be called the patient mobility, that lighting of the pipe with a directed, deliberate, parsimonious, subconscious purpose which is to be found in the smoking adept can be acquired only by long habit, even by a sort of probity. Between the smoker and his pipe there is much the same osmosis as exists between a painter and his painting. No artist has ever treated a pipe as merely an object of still life. The pipe is alive—especially when it is alight—and Baudelaire's phrase is full of a profound significance, "You will attribute to your pipe the strange faculty of *smoking you*." (Vous attribuerez à votre pipe l'étrange faculté de *vous fumer*.) The italics, it should be added, are his.

That is why we can never repeat too often that though one may be a born smoker, one single essay at smoking is not enough, persistence is needful that will slowly ripen into a pleasure that ever becomes more living, more perfected.

For the smoker and his pipe have to do with the weather, an element or number of elements full of surprises, an element that can never be understood other than relatively, that is capricious, barometric. Tobacco smoke takes the color of the weather and will taste of it. The smoker and his pipe are at once the bene-

ficiaries and the victims of the sky, the wind, the rain—the weather.
They attempt to be its master, knowing full well that they are
its slaves.

Besides these unforeseeable elements the smoker and his pipe
are ever situated between two alternatives or alternations—the
pipe getting too hot or going out altogether. If it gets too hot
he has the agony of fear as the heat penetrates the wall of the
bowl in his fingers; if it goes out there is the misery of seeing
the tobacco become dead. There is a debatable axiom that once a
pipe goes out it should not be relit—debatable, we say, for it
depends upon what point the combustion had reached when it
died; if it was soon after lighting the case is less serious.

These alternatives or alternations are clearly and absolutely
opposed to one another. It is only reasonable to suppose that it
should be possible to attain something between the two, for ideal
drawing on the pipe would obviate the mischief in either case
and solve the problem. But this is simplifying the situation too
easily, for there is no such thing as ideal drawing, and this reasonable halfway line can be obtained between the vector of overheating and the vector of extinction only by a sort of regulating
alternation round the midway line; that is to say by drawing on
the pipe in puffs more or less heavy and more or less frequent
according to the supposed state of combustion.

The portion between the burning surface of the tobacco after
lighting and the dottle at the bottom of the bowl is what one
might call the sacred space, the holy of holies, and it demands our
utmost solicitude, our entire attention, for that is where the perfect smoke comes from, and it will only give us of its best in
proportion as we give of our best to it. This is where science
quits the realm of theory, passing from the limits of the conscious
to penetrate the subconscious. This can be done only when the
organs of the mouth have acquired its precepts. It must, more-

over, be emphasized that this acquired science, this knowledge, must become mechanical, as, for instance, the *vibrato* of a wind instrument in a jazz band, for only when it is thus mechanical and intuitive can it be understood or acquired.

Superheating and going out—between these alternatives the smoker has no choice. The damper the tobacco the worse the situation if the pipe goes out. The nicotine, which vaporizes at 250° C., forms a deposit as soon as this degree of incandescence is reached; it cannot help doing so and that is why it is as risky to activate combustion as to relight a pipe that has gone out, if the pipe is still hot. This deposit, or rather the fall of nicotine on tobacco not yet smoked, is what is chiefly to be feared, for what was once something to charm then turns into a rank poison.

There is a certain theoretical or imaginary stage at which the smoker can relax his drawing, and another, equally imaginary, when the heat alternation has less likelihood of causing damage; and the first stage having been passed it is permissible to accelerate the drawing, all the more since the combustion itself accelerates it, for the smoke caused by the drawing passing through the tobacco charges it with an even greater humidity. But it is precisely then, in this center that impinges on both these stages that the pipe, by the degree of its aroma, attains the maximum of its exquisiteness. There is no need to emphasize the difficulty of systematizing this operation, for one is dealing with a living—or semi-living—object.

The supreme art would be to exercise a gradual slackening of drawing as the emanence of the tobacco becomes richer, more nourished, more affirmative, and by that sort of adroitness or inner sense that rarely fails the smoker, realize that the upper surface of the dottle is being reached and combustion can be maintained by a few more vigorous whiffs. On knocking out the

pipe it will be found that the ash reveals how well the pipe has
been smoked. The pipe has to be lifted, so to speak, as a horse
is lifted before taking a hurdle or ditch.

After some twenty years of experience we have reached the
point where, after smoking, our pipe-bowl yields nothing but fine
ash, with one or two minute shreds of tobacco at the very bottom.
In this case the dottle is merely a hypothetical term to clarify
the test, for the good smoker burns his dottle with the rest.

Taking no account of the satisfaction this gives, a result such as
this is no less economical than gratifying. When one reckons the
number of dottles that were too closely packed, or badly made,
which have not burned or have been shifted from their proper
position, it can be appreciated how many smokes have been
spoiled or lost, how many odoriferous particles that cried aloud
to live have never so much as been born, how great a cloud of
aroma has never reached the nostrils. Two or three extra puffs
at a pipe—even if they be slightly less delightful than those that
have gone before—are not to be disdained, either for themselves
or for the good they do to the base of the bowl by consuming
the dottle.

Of course the smoker who has not become the slave of his
pipe can break off a smoke when he likes; but we disagree
with this and maintain that the thing to do is to fill the bowl
only half full. There is nothing more vexatious than being obliged
to put out a pipe. We are all slaves to something however trivial
it may be, and life consists in passing on, and posing to oneself, only
such problems as actually touch on our freedom. We should be
much too grieved, suffer too great a remorse if we had to empty our
pipe bowls of still smokable tobacco.

GENERALITIES

The damper tobacco which forms the dottle is not confined to the base of the bowl but in a much lesser degree it clings to the walls. This can be verified by examining a lighted pipe; the tobacco burns clear in the center, but as it gets near the bowl it becomes increasingly dull. By bad smoking this can reduce a pipe to the condition shown below, where only a small hole is left for the tobacco to burn, an epicenter as it were. The formation of this side dottle is an inexorable law and no fault

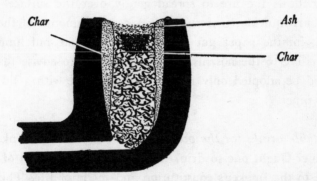

of the pipe, and it is vain to seek a remedy for it. It is there that the fibro-granular exchange takes place between the grain of the wood and the constituents of the tobacco. The essential thing is to see that the pipe is lit properly; the rest must be left to remedy itself according to the seasoning of the pipe and the skill of the smoker.

A new pipe grows hot more quickly than a seasoned one, so there is no cause for alarm if it becomes very hot when first smoked; this will rectify itself by degrees. The best thing to do is to reduce the strength and frequency of the puffs. On the first sign of the pipe going out, smooth the surface of the tobacco with the thumb, press the latter tightly over the top of the bowl, and draw several times quickly and frequently, removing the thumb as soon as the pipe seems fairly alight.

To stabilize the combustion and slacken it without risking putting out the pipe, take something with a flat surface—such as a box of matches, the palm of the hand, or the ball of the thumb—and keep it pressed over the bowl until the pipe is alight; this is a method much used by experienced smokers.

According to certain adepts in the art of smoking, the best thing for this purpose is a piece of coarse paper with a hole in it, placed over the bowl and kept there by the smoker's fingers. Considerable experience has proved the efficacy of this method, which allows the fire to spread gently over the surface rather than burn quickly. Unfortunately a certain amount of the taste is lost, for the paper not only taints the smoke but hinders it from rising to the nostrils. We would therefore advise that this method be adopted only in the open air, and with a lid fitted to the pipe.

Suitable drinks for the occasion. What should be drunk when smoking? Ought one to drink at all? Is there any form of drink suited to the smoker's constitution and mode of life? These are questions that at first sight seem of secondary importance and outside the scope of this treatise.

Sufficient to say that a wet mouth is better than a dry one, a good meal better than a poor, a healthy appetite better than a feeble one. Rum, beer, tea, coffee are all suitable drinks to go with smoking. It must be admitted that the smell of a pipe and the smell of rum go well together, for both are the products of wood; there are sympathies between living feelings and affinities between inanimate things. Nor can it be denied that alcohol is sympathetic to smoke, and milk the very reverse. Alcohol favors the action of tobacco but milk neutralizes it; the one is ardent, the other passive; it is possible that they are complementary.

The smoker has an immense gamut to cover, the gamut of an entire life; he can let his imagination run riot as he waits upon circumstances to offer subjects for experiment.

Had this matter of drink none but a personal interest for us we would pass on with the remark that it is of too general a nature to devote much consideration to; the pipe itself is an admirable digestive and a no less delightful aperitif; it is full of adventure, and the matter of drinking and eating must be left to masters such as Brillat Savarin, whose *Physiology of Taste* will supply any *lacunae* in our remarks.

Where should one smoke? Theoretically in a closed place where a still atmosphere favors combustion and makes a sort of secondary wall to the bowl of the pipe, retaining the effluences and allowing none of them to be lost—the profound osmosis between the pipe and its surroundings. The bowl becomes the center of the world, the point where the radiating circles of the real and the unreal meet. Do not smoke too near a fireplace, door or window, and do not move about too suddenly as this creates a draught by displacement unless the thumb be first placed over the bowl or the latter sheltered by the open hand to prevent the phenomenon of eduction. Of the three illustrations only the first two portray an acceptable condition, the movement in the second suggesting a slight zephyr that might waft the smoke to the nostrils. But in no circumstances must one walk too quickly when smoking a pipe, not only because of the effect on combustion but also from the point of view of health. An athlete may well be a pipe smoker, but he does not smoke when in training.

In fine weather one can smoke fruitfully by an open window, provided the door or other windows in the room are closed; this applies equally to a car or railway carriage so long as the window is lowered only a little. The smoker will learn by experience how far he can go. If one happens to be out walking on a windy day, a tree trunk or the lee of a wall—even a slope in the ground—will partially break the force of the wind and afford shelter for smoking. The thumb placed over the bowl will keep out drops of rain; but if one is out on a wet day it is advisable to smoke with the bowl upside down, as many smokers invariably do in the open air. If the pipe has been properly filled there will be little likelihood of any burning particles dropping out. Needless to say, this should not be made a habit.

Practically speaking it does not matter where one smokes. A smoker who enjoys life will enjoy his pipe anywhere and everywhere, in all places, temperatures and circumstances. He will learn to appreciate it in sunshine, or shadow, cold or damp, by the camp fire, after a bath, in a bath. A pipe in the rain can attain to the sublime; a change of temperature may make it sing, weep, laugh, get lightheaded, endowing its aroma with something of a lively spirit. Experiences such as these are hidden from the wise and prudent, from the practical man and the theorist alike; let one such talk to a sailor and appreciate what he has to learn. The pipe is life to the seafaring man, and with his "nose-warmer" he gets near the inspiration of his being; he knows that the taste of a short pipe is in harmony with the taste of the sea and with the course of his fortunes.*

The man who suffers from boredom should smoke cigarettes, a pipe is not for him.

Let us close these remarks with the axiom: Every smoker invents his own way of smoking.

* It may be observed in this connection that in scientific astrology (*sic*) the Moon, mistress of all journeys by sea, reigns also over tobacco.

EMPTYING A PIPE

If a pipe has been charged according to rule, and the contents smoked to the very end, in principle it should empty completely when the bowl is turned upside down. In practice the emptying is not completed without one or two light taps with the hand on the base of the bowl. This additional operation is easier with a clay or porcelain pipe, as the tobacco clings less to the walls of the bowl, but on the other hand it is a riskier thing to do as they are so fragile. It is harder to empty a well-seasoned and charred pipe than a new one, for not taking into account the narrowness of the bowl, the charred surface is always quick to become moist under the action of the pyrogenic products of to-bacco and its own colloidal nature, and has a tendency to hold in the ash and stop it falling from the bowl. The drawing below illustrates this clearly.

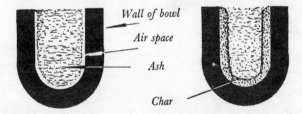

Wall of bowl

Air space

Ash

Char

The problem of the dottle is more difficult. Even in a new pipe it will resist being knocked out, partly on account of its nicotinic nature and partly because it has been drawn to the interior orifice of the channel, which we saw in the drawing on page 9, where certain of its constituents have adhered or been drawn in by the suction of smoking. However, if the pipe has been filled according to rule, a few taps should suffice to dislodge the dottle.

On no account should the pipe be emptied by knocking it

sharply against some hard object, and this for various cogent reasons. If you happen to do this in a restaurant you will summon the waiter needlessly; secondly, and more important, you will risk sooner or later knocking off the top of the bowl. To get rid of this dottle of unsmoked tobacco that clings to the walls of the bowl, the best thing to use is a penknife or some similar pointed implement. This method, as sensible as it is speedy, is preferable to repeated and even more vigorous knocking of the bowl against the heel of the shoe, a habit with many wearers of crepe-rubber soles; for more often than one would suspect this snaps the ebonite mouthpiece, if not the wooden stem (as shown below).

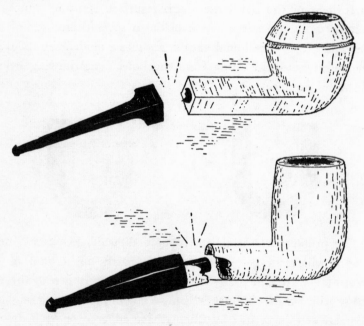

The briar pipe has the reputation—especially among those who do not smoke one—of being strong. According to the way it is originally cut, as we have seen, it is often composed of a congeries of knots that work into a sort of vortex that breaks more easily than ordinary wood tissue. In the mass these knots are very resistant, but they are unyielding and crack easily. The crack is usually clean and rarely penetrates more than halfway; but it is clear that the briar is almost as fragile as the clay pipe. It needs to be treated with as much care as a clay, meerschaum or porcelain pipe; that is, at least, an excellent principle upon which to go.

Tobacconists sell ash trays in the shape of an upside down lid, from the center of which protrudes a large knob. A layer of rubber, or other elastic material such as cork, surrounds this knob. This offers a practical method of cleaning one's pipe, by taking it by the bowl and tapping it against the knob—the ash tray itself collecting the ashes; but this has the same danger as knocking a pipe out on the sole of a crepe shoe. Except for thick pipes, in most cases there is a risk of breakage, chipping and other annoying accidents. There is, therefore, between the sole and the knob, only the difference of the law of least effort. It's only by virtue of this law that the knob is superior to the sole. Consequently, we recommend neither one nor the other.

The entire contents of the bowl can be easily ejected by means of a simple nail file that will also detach any particles of tobacco clinging to the walls. In doing this the little finger may well play its part, always provided that the bowl is big enough to admit it.

To sum up, it is better to empty the bowl by scraping than by knocking it out; but if the latter method be chosen for one reason or another, the palm of the hand should be used. If the pipe then breaks or cracks, the smoker may attribute it to bad luck rather than to his own fault.

The quality or state of the tobacco may also affect the emptying of the bowl, and in this connection let us hear what Conan Doyle says, in *The Sign of Four:*

"Yes, I have been guilty of several monographs [says Sherlock Holmes]. They are all upon technical subjects. Here, for example, is one 'Upon the Distinction Between the Ashes of the Various Tobaccos.' In it I enumerate a hundred and forty forms of cigar, cigarette, and pipe tobacco, with colored plates illustrating the difference in the ash. It is a point which is continually turning up in criminal trials, and which is sometimes of supreme importance as a clue. If you can say definitely, for example, that some murder has been done by a man who is smoking an Indian lunkah, it obviously narrows your field of search. To the trained eye there is as much difference between the black ash of a Trichinopoly and the white fluff of bird's-eye as there is between a cabbage and a potato."

CLEANING

We shall take advantage of our remarks on this subject to clear up once and for all the question of the "smelly pipe," so often a matter of reproach by nonsmokers.

This smell is occasioned solely by the negligence of smokers who fail to take care of their pipes, even walking about with quantities of cold, stale nicotine in their pockets, which exhale a fetid stench that is attributed by the ignorant to the innocent pipe instead of to a culpable lack of hygiene on the part of the smoker. The smell permeates every shred of their clothing, clinging especially to woolen garments, and reaches even the skin itself—and a lighted pipe only augments the smell instead of quenching it.

A smelly smoker means a bad smoker; this is a truth that should be taught as an axiom for the protection of good smokers. In principle it may be extended even to nonsmokers who neglect their persons!

A chemical explanation will make these matters clear. When two or three successive combustions take place in a pipe, the mouthpiece, if the smoker has neglected to clean it, becomes filled with a fluid that has an alkaline smell so potent that it will drive to a distance the most experienced and hardiest of smokers. This fluid is composed to a very small degree—and then only in bent mouthpieces—of saliva, induced in quantities by smoking a dirty pipe. The smoker's breath also plays a part in the composition of this fluid, for he has had to breathe hard through the mouthpiece to keep his dirty pipe alight. Another constituent is water.

Tobacco being a substance eminently hydrophilous, or eager for water, it is more or less humid according to the hygrometric state of the atmosphere. When moist tobacco burns (and tobacco is always to a certain degree moist) the water it contains vaporizes in the bowl of the pipe, and when condensing on the colder inner surface of the channel of the mouthpiece, it mixes with the fluid mentioned above. The most interesting part of this fluid is composed of tar, to a greater or less degree, and four alkaline substances of which the best known is nicotine.

As these tar particles, which are the product of the pyrogenous decomposition of vegetable substances, only form in appreciable quantities if the tobacco burns badly, through improper drawing or too great humidity, a portion of them will be decomposed and not burned.

The four bases mentioned above are:

Nicotine ($C_{10}H_{14}Az_2$).
Nicotinine, an isomere.
Two other alkaloids—$C_{10}H_{12}Az_2$ and $C_{10}H_{10}Az_2$.

Nicotine itself is a colorless fluid with a nauseous smell, especially when hot. It occurs in tobacco in the proportion of 1-8 per cent; the other bases are in the proportion of 5/1,000, 20/1,000, 1/1,000.

The so-called bad smell of a pipe can be avoided by never

smoking it when already hot; indeed, this ought not to be done in any case from the point of view of combustion as much as to avoid the bad smell. But the sovereign and only true remedy is constant and regular cleaning of the pipe.

PARTIAL CLEANING.   It is not enough to clean out the bowl only. It is for this reason that pipe cleaners have been made of strands of wire into which is twisted some absorbent material. The cleaner is passed through the mouthpiece and stem, much as one cleans the barrel of a gun. It should be revolved as it is pulled back and forth, then withdrawn and thrown away; though it may be used again if only the portion that has penetrated the orifice of the bowl has got soiled. Some smokers put the pipe cleaners to dry for further use, but economical though this may be, it is not hygienic.

Every pipe ought to be cleaned directly after smoking so that it will be ready for use again. A well-kept pipe cannot smell other than nice. Some smokers recognize their pipes solely by the smell, even when they are empty. Every pipe has its own individual smell which does not vanish when it is cleaned. The reputation of smelling bad is based upon a prejudice, and as we have seen this bad reputation belongs rather to the negligence of the smoker than to the pipe itself. The smell of cold nicotine is bearable, but as soon as it becomes hot it is abominable. One can imagine what a fetid stench may be evoked by smoking a pipe that is never cleaned, the nicotine stagnating as smoke follows smoke until the entire container is poisoned through and through. Solidified in their filth these poisonous elements come alive as each successive smoke liquefies and adds to their nastiness; one can hear them groaning and bubbling at the bottom of the bowl as though unable to support their own obscenity.

It may happen that a single smoke will cause in a pipe this unpleasant agglomeration of liquid and solid—even gaseous—

matter. The pipe cleaner must then be used before the combustion proceeds further. Pipes with bent stems or curved mouthpieces are more subject to this mischief than others. It will be necessary, therefore, to employ a stricter regime of cleaning for such pipes than is called for by others. If this proves ineffective, it means

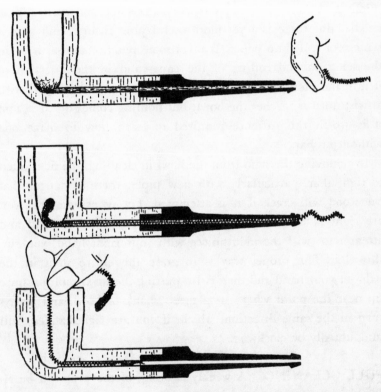

that the pipe is a bad one—nicotinic, it is called—and must be thrown away. All this may happen from very obscure causes that it would be interesting and profitable to investigate, especially when briars of perfectly normal shape and make are affected with this unforeseen and incurable poisoning. Instances of this occur often enough to make it proper to emphasize their existence to smoke who may not have come across them.

The pipe cleaner is a most valuable implement for partial cleaning, all the more so when, instead of being pushed up and down the stem, it is used in the manner illustrated by us in the drawing on page 127. The same excellent result can, of course, be obtained by several different objects. In spring, for instance, if you are taking a country walk you will find long grasses that are suitable. A hen's feather is equally efficacious, or even a pine needle. But there is a yet more useful pipe cleaner, and that is a piece of rolled-up paper. It takes some practice to use, both in the selection and rolling of the paper and in the insertion of it into the mouthpiece, where it should be pushed forward with a twist until it reaches the bowl; but nothing comes up to it, and it is worth the patience required to learn how to make one without mishap.

In removing the stem from the bowl in cleaning, the fit is often so tight that, particularly with new pipes, there is danger that the wood will crack if it is attempted. Let us assume that you are right-handed. If you hold the bowl in your left hand and attempt to twist the mouthpiece with your right hand, you run this risk. The proper way is to grasp the entire stem in the palm of your hand and then twist, putting the maximum pressure up near the point where stem meets shank of bowl, and always turn in the same direction, which, if you are right-handed, will undoubtedly be clockwise.

FULL CLEANING. A weekly cleaning of the pipe can be effected with rum or some other natural and aromatic form of alcohol, but we do not really approve of the introduction of alcohol into the pipe, and even less of any sweet liquid. The latter should most certainly be avoided on account of the saccharine content. All the same, it is better to use alcohol than to take the pipe to pieces too often, as this is apt to cause a weakness at the junction of the wood and ebonite. Perhaps one might alternate the methods. The best way to apply alcohol is to take a mouth-ful of rum and blow it with all one's force down the mouthpiece so that it comes out at the bowl, which must be held upside down.* As an extension of this procedure it is possible to make the rum bubble in the bowl by blowing gently through the mouthpiece, in this instance, of course, keeping the bowl the right way up. When doing this it is better to wrap a piece of rag round the outside of the bowl to preserve the patina in case the liquid overflows. When all has been done, the pipe should be allowed to dry, a pipe cleaner being passed through it before filling the bowl for another smoke.

There is considerable difference of opinion about methods of cleaning a pipe. Some advocate alcohol at 90 per cent proof, others condemn it utterly. Brandy of any mark from the current year to Napoleon brandy have been suggested and may be tried. Some hold by pure water; others eau de cologne which, they insist, makes the best possible bath. So long as each is followed by quick drying any one of these methods may be adopted, for it is the cleaning that is the important thing. So the smoker may choose whatever he feels is best for him and his pipes.

These partial cleanings find their consummation in

TOTAL CLEANING, to which the smoker should turn his atten-tion every month or two according to the number of his pipes. Each should be taken to pieces for a scrupulous overhaul with rag, pipe cleaner and alcohol, not forgetting a piece of flannel or chamois leather for the final polish-up. The purpose of this cleaning is to get every part of the pipe completely dry, a sort of airing of all the interior portions of the pipe. It is good to expose them when apart to good fresh air, and to delay smoking

* It has been known for the rum, having reached the smoker's mouth, to have been put to some purpose other than pipe cleaning.

as long as possible. In this way you will have in your pocket
or hanging in the pipe rack a collection of healthy and lively
pipes that will do you credit.

SEASONING

Seasoning is the fruit of long and exacting labor, a sort of combustion that is at once permanent and intermittent, which means
that however beautiful a pipe may be in its seasoning, it is always in process of becoming yet more so. Seasoning is to smoking
what artistic labor is to the poet—by mutual working, a rhythm,
a sort of marriage between the two, an equilibrium is reached
that produces a poem—and brings a pipe to maturity.

PRELIMINARIES TO SEASONING.   Sorely as we are tempted
to do so we may not condemn as beyond right of appeal the
preparation of a pipe by the application of rum, brandy—choice
or otherwise—of alcohols of any nature whatsoever. Alcohol is the
friend of tobacco; but is it the friend of wood, particularly of the
briar root? It may bring out the beauty of the grain but only at
the price of its rapid deterioration. Alcohol (Arabic *kohol*) is a
word employed by the Arabs to describe a subtle thing that
intoxicates, that attacks, that harms the throat, that excites everything it touches. It is the *enfant terrible* of beverages, the snake
in the grass among liquors. Alcohol requires as much care in its
preparation as tobacco. They are two products, one liquid and
the other solid, apt to stir up the animal spirits by direct, healthy
and natural action. Just as tobacco gives something to the pipe
in which it is consumed, so does alcohol give something of itself
to the receptacle in which it is stored. The spirits of brandy
acquire the clearness of cognac when matured in an acacia cask.
We cannot, therefore, treat this deity offhandedly, and deny its

qualities as a preseasoner, so to speak, for the pipe. But alcohol must be employed only with the utmost caution and economy.

The preliminary seasoning by alcohol at least ensures the removal of any varnish there may be and scours away the polish from the interior of the bowl, at the same time modifying the harshness of the wood before it has been subjected to a "baptism by fire." It is a sort of deflowering of the pipe, taking away its virginity; on the introduction of a foreign body (in this instance tobacco) the virgin wood reacts and labors, seeking to adjust itself to what is demanded of it. Alcohol being, as it were, midway between liquid and fire—or perhaps more exactly an unlit fire—is the medium that enables the pipe to accept what is placed within it.

We do most strongly reprehend the expedient of filling the bowl to the brim with any sort of alcohol and setting light to it. This is an act of vandalism that may or may not achieve its purpose but is not the less to be condemned wholeheartedly. A pipe is not an omelette. A wood pipe should never be submitted, on the pretext that it is more resistant, to any shock that would not be applied to one of more delicate material, such as meerschaum. We have seen this procedure carried to the point of insanity; at the moment when the alcohol, having burned down to the bottom of the bowl, showed signs of flickering out, the vandal blew down the mouthpiece to make the alcohol bubble and fan the flame; and so the mischief was completed. The wooden pipe bowl might have been a glass retort for all the difference that was made between them.

If you wish to intoxicate your pipe before firing it—the anæsthetic of the operating room, or the condemned man's nip of brandy—block up the end of the mouthpiece with a wooden plug cut for the purpose, fill the bowl with choice alcoholic liquor, and set it down in some safe place where it cannot be disturbed by mistake or accident. In less than a week the wood will have absorbed every particle of the alcohol; peaceful penetration, it may be called. If this method seems too drastic, soak a rag in the alcohol and with the tip of the finger wipe it round and round the inside of the bowl.

If alcohol seems unsuitable for this sort of thing, a light pre-seasoning may be administered by applying a little salad oil to the interior of the bowl and leaving it for a week before smoking the pipe. In any event, it is strongly recommended to remove the polish from the inside of the bowl, especially if it be a pipe of some special make with a fine name to it, one that has been got up for the public and does not reach the smoker in the simple state it left the craftsman's hands.

The use of any of these preparations is better than the method adopted more frequently than we care to remember which consists in stuffing tobacco, no matter how roughly, right up to the top of an unsmoked pipe, lighting up, and blowing down the mouthpiece, to the accompaniment of a shower of sparks in proportion to the force of the blower's lungs, until all the tobacco is burned. After such a desecration there are grooves and craters all over the interior wall of the bowl, and the ebonite has become soft and loose in its wooden housing in the stem. If you light a match and hold the ebonite plug in the flame, turning it rapidly for two or three seconds so it doesn't melt or catch fire, it will soften enough so that if you then press it head-on against a hard surface, its circumference will expand. It usually does so exactly enough to make a tight fit again. There are pipe quacks who say "Your pipe seasoned in an hour," much as others advertise "A splendid head of hair in a week."

Some simple soul may imagine that he can entrust the seasoning of his pipe to someone else, but this is to betray ignorance of the whole point of seasoning. The pleasure of smoking a pipe comes as much from seasoning it as from the aroma it exhales.

The two are inseparable; indeed, it is rare to find a man who cares to smoke another fellow's pipe.

Beginners show a remarkable ingenuity in their early attempts at preseasoning. Some remove the interior polish with emery paper, others scrape the bowl out thoroughly with the blade of a kitchen knife, others promote combustion with the bellows, others have recourse to a vacuum cleaner, and yet others take the bowl in a pair of tongs and hold it over the flame of a fire or a candle, or even a gas burner. It is a common practice to pass a red-hot knitting needle down the mouthpiece, thus causing a peculiarly unpleasant smell of burning rubber. Needless to say, the victims of these atrocities seldom recover. But what matters that to such lunatics! They start all over again with a fresh pipe, maybe even smoking a cigarette as they do so. It is true, their purpose was to smoke a pipe; but to what purpose!

At this point we ought to state that there are certain mechanical processes of seasoning; without casting any doubts on their efficacy we can but hope that they will not be adopted commercially.

SEASONING PROPER.   In whatever way a pipe may be treated its proper seasoning must follow certain rules which, without being rigid, are such that the smoker must abide by them. The procedure of making the wood absorb alcohol, which is the only pre-seasoning we can countenance beyond the removal of polish, etc., does not dispense with certain precautions that must be taken during the early smokes. These are slight; at first it is common prudence that must take precedence over pleasure, if pleasure is the object in view. The first five or six pipes should be only a quarter filled; the next ten or so half filled; a few more three quarters filled, and then five or six barely filled— and always according to the proper manner of filling, but somewhat lightly.

Lighting these incomplete charges will be more troublesome and the smoking of them less orthodox. It matters little; before long the bowl will have taken on a certain fullness of figure and the charring will increase in arithmetical progression with the number of pipes smoked. This system of filling by stages is excellent in the sense that, contrary to what one would expect, it furthers the homogeneity of the approaching seasoning; the top of the bowl always seasons and chars sooner than the bottom by virtue of the more violent burning produced by lighting the pipe. The phenomenon can easily be verified; if the bowl of a seasoned pipe be scraped with a penknife it will be found that the deposit at the top is black to a considerable depth whilst at the bottom the wood itself will appear after a touch or two with the blade, especially if the pipe has been seasoned by an amateur.

The charring at the bottom of the bowl is better when the pipe is filled by the stages mentioned above and, what is more, an appreciable part of the wood stem has followed its example, by what might be called capillary action. All this is an excellent preparation for smokes to come. The filling in stages is particularly recommended for porcelain pipes which, being thicker at the base, have less chance of breaking. It is even advisable to make the stages more gradual with them than with the briar. Every part of the pipe will gain by doing so.

A virgin pipe is more fragile than a mature one; it certainly weighs less. If you put your pipe on the scales when you buy it, and again when the bowl is so charred that it needs scraping out, you will perceive the difference in weight. This comes from the charred matter* and the penetration of the tar particles which solidify in the tissue of the wood. On lighting, you awaken a world of sensitivity that asks only to give, asks only that you draw from it, and this, as the Mystics teach us, is but another

* There is no common term for the charred substance in a pipe, and henceforth in these pages it will be called "char."

aspect of self-sacrifice. That is what happens when your lighted match arouses this world of eager yielding in your pipe.

Even a well-seasoned pipe demands attentive, scrupulous cleaning, careful smoking. A pipe has a life of its own, an independent existence. One never knows what it will yield, what it is capable of exhaling or imagining. Seasoning is unceasing, a never-completed process, and even when arrested it still waits to be resumed. It is only by thinking of it as such a process never achieved that one accepts it in all its implications; no smoker would venture to say what are its limits, for they have little to do with the pipe's maturity, which is in itself an indefinable condition. To those who dispute our advice on the different stages of filling a pipe during seasoning we would advise a full charge but loosely packed. It will be at their own risk and peril.

OTHER MATTERS

The char in a pipe is, in principle, the product of the marriage of tobacco and wood fiber. It is to tobacco what tannin is to wine. Without a good cask wine loses its bouquet, it is not itself, sometimes it turns acid and denatures. Char is a superficial

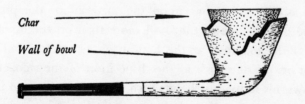

Char

Wall of bowl

product, the sweat of a pipe, one might call it if the term be not taken in a pejorative sense, that deposits itself on the internal walls of the bowl. This is very obvious when one has by mischance broken a porcelain pipe or the well-seasoned bowl of a briar; the char being a harder substance, but less ductile, resists the shock and simply comes away, as shown on page 135.

In a briar pipe the union of the tobacco and the wood is closer, and it may be stated that another char exists—the inner or char proper. Being below the superficial char it serves as a bed for the latter, not so much united with it as placed in juxtaposition to it. It is between these two kinds of char that lies the seat where exchange is made between the moving tobacco and the stationary fiber—the place of mystery where the ordinary char has its origins.

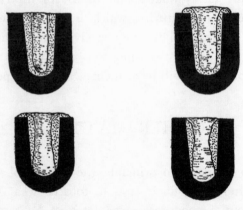

Chars are of many different kinds: those shown here and on the next page are but a few. They depend as much upon the idiosyncrasies of the smoker as upon the material of the pipe; they may be on one side of the bowl more than on the other, bulge more at the top than at the bottom or vice versa; and all this for various reasons such as the disposition of the smoker's teeth and jaws, his individual habits such as bending down to light up, or smoking more frequently in the open, living in a windy place —there is no end to the causes. Some chars take a descending form, others an ascending (as shown above). These can be caused by any of the aforementioned reasons or from the homogeneity or heterogeneity of the fibers in the knots—we are here dealing with briars and not such capricious materials as corncob or asbes-

tos. But all these questions are of secondary importance. An uneven char proves nothing to the discredit of the pipe or the

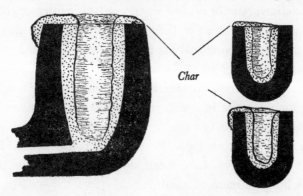

Char

smoker. It just makes one charm more.* The pipe's structure in
itself permits of these refinements of behavior; there are func-
tional chars and adventurous chars; their diversity makes a world
that defies investigation. It is interesting to see how a man seasons
his pipe. It presents something of the analogy of perfume; a
woman always thinks her neighbor's perfume better than her
own, and the other man's seasoning is always what one envies for
one's own pipes.

The ordinary char being superficial, in juxtaposition to the char
proper, it follows that the latter should receive our chief attention; it forms an integral part of the pipe and is the source of its
taste—it is not a mere waste product.

While on this subject, we are always rather distrustful of virgin
pipes that smell too good at the first smoking. They do not always
live up to their promise, as if the anachronism of their virginal
excellence had been put to the debit of future smokes. Sometimes
they turn "sulky" when, having been laid aside for some weeks,

* When the top of the bowl of a pipe has been made uneven in pattern
(as above) the char has a tendency to collect on the lower portion as the
illustration shows. This is aggravated if the mouthpiece is curved, especially
if the smoker is accustomed to taking his pipe when out walking.

they are picked up again to smoke. Have we not all of us on occasion thrown out as useless pipes that, after some twenty smokes, refuse to draw, remain shut in on themselves, neuter or cold, with poker faces? Leave them to their sulks for three months or six— even a year. Something will happen; suddenly they will open out and become good. This is a mystery that needs clearing up, say you. Let us not delve further into the matter, for it will make subject for a treatise in itself; yet even then the truth will never come out, it will be but the turning over of blank leaves if we divorce this behavior from its poetic inconsequence. Learned men, it would seem, have been no more explicit in their researches into the sense of smell.

SCRAPING OUT THE BOWL

This title is self-explanatory—scraping the interior of the bowl free of its char. So long as he knows what he is about the expert smoker cannot make a mistake. Scraping out is an operation much less delicate than that of lighting a pipe, its combustion, or its cleaning. In the first place it implies that the pipe is "ripe" and consequently less easily broken; having withstood many shocks it can now be treated more brusquely. But this does not mean one should go to work as with a pickax but by careful scraping, as one might use in peeling an apple or pear. The object is to obtain an even surface within the bowl, as when the pipe was new, and this is of supreme importance for subsequent smokes.

The operation should be performed slowly, gently, in a good light so that the whole of the bowl can be inspected. It does not matter what implement is used so long as the blade is narrow and strong. The interior of the bowl ought to be left in the same shape, though naturally of somewhat smaller caliber, as it was when new.

But here a problem arises—a much debated problem among ·pipe scrapers. To what degree should a pipe be scraped out? There are two schools of thought on this subject.

The First School of Thought recommends chipping out the char in pieces, starting from the lip of the bowl. With a little experience it is easy to do this right to the bottom. The interior of the bowl will now appear of a shiny blackness, for we are in the presence of the char proper, which must not be touched. It will be sufficient from time to time to turn the pipe upside down to let the loosened char fall out, and when this has all been got rid of, a gentle blowing through the mouthpiece will disperse any powder or small fragments remaining. Nothing now is left to do but clean up, and refill the bowl.

The Second School of Thought believes in a partial scraping out, for it holds that leaving a thin coat of char makes a better foundation for future smokes. It is impossible to obtain a new pipe, they say, by scraping out an old one; and a partial scraping gives all the result required. Char is formed of a series of successive deposits of various strata and coalescences that create the fragrance of the pipe. A film is deposited with each smoke, a new combination or marriage, as it were, of wood and tobacco. Partial scraping eases the pipe of some of its burden and renews its taste, at the same time retaining a good basis for future combustion. In short, such a partial scraping out minimizes the danger of overheating.

Each of these schools of thought has many points in its favor, but having tried them out, turn and turn about, for some years, we ourselves hold by neither. On the contrary we favor a

Third School of Thought, which recommends what will be called curetting, its purpose being to prevent the superficial char from forming. The bowl is scraped out several times a week, or even

every day after the pipe has been smoked. The frequency will depend on the nature of the pipe and the habits of the smoker.*
The essential thing is to keep an eye on the char to prevent its forming, in other words, to make the pipe "toe the line."

This ideal procedure, according to our way of thinking, would go against the grain with many inveterate smokers who are proud of the charred condition of their pipes. Indeed, it is not too much to say that not a few of them get less pleasure from their smoking than from watching their pipes season; for in its seasoning lies the honor and glory of a pipe, the proof of its perfect combustion, the crowning of an art that is at once patient and unconstrained, of a consummate virtuosity. It is the tangible fruit of labor, and its absence would be to the smoker what the taking away of the cast of his masterpiece would be to the sculptor if he were left with nothing but the mold. One needs to have the coveted char left in the body of the pipe.

It is needful to bow to facts; a scraped-out pipe will never taste as good as it did when charring up; it then attained a plenitude of savor that it cannot yield when the char has been scraped out. Some smokers are so convinced of this that when the bowl of a pipe gets too charred to be scraped out, they put it aside and get a new one. We have long been the proud and courageous apostle of the school that holds that charring should never get to the stage of closing the bowl.

CURETTING is then a middle term between—and combining—the two schools of thought. It is the surest guarantee of long life to a pipe. It maintains its fragrance; perpetuates its virginity; and makes the pipe almost as good after many years' service as it was the day it was acquired, thus demonstrating that curetting is an

---

* Like the cigarette smoker, the pipe lover may be a light, medium or heavy smoker. What cannot be said of him is that he "lights one pipe from another."

economy as much to the senses as to the purse (especially for those smokers who throw away their old pipes). It is where experience encourages and gives birth to faith.

However, let not the votary of either of the two first-mentioned schools be troubled if the setting forth of our third system has induced him to abandon what once he held so dear and by which he lived; his pipe will season just the same, both with its char proper and with the venerable patina that is the joy and honor of every true smoker. He may also accept the fact that to char up inside proves nothing. A pipe that comes to be scraped out for the tenth or twentieth time loses nothing of its elegant proportions, its nobility of appearance. On the contrary, it is superior to a pipe that has been scraped out but once. What is to be said, then, of a pipe that has no need to be scraped out at all, thanks to the procedure we are now advocating? It is like those centenarians whom we call hale and hearty, like the oak in springtime. No trace of decrepitude, firm as a rock, resplendent with the light of eternity —that light that only Nature can sometimes open our eyes to behold. It would therefore be foolish to cling to an appearance to the detriment of a reality which in substance and appearance alike leaves nothing to be desired.

Nevertheless we cannot refrain from words of advice to smokers who still cleave to the first two categories and refuse to abandon their methods and habits. Our remarks are of general interest, so that we may retain the attention of all fervent pipe smokers, whatever their habits or the kind of pipes they smoke—or their views on scraping out. It is dangerous to cling to the notion that a pipe should be scraped out only *in extremis;* this encourages it to split or crack, particularly if it is very charred up and smoked with tobacco that is too moist. The cherrywood is especially subject to this phenomenon, although its bark exterior should preserve it. Clay pipes are even more susceptible.

The smoker will never find his pipe bowl completely charred

up, but filling it will become increasingly difficult, especially if carried out properly. We have seen some smokers obliged to stuff in tobacco with a pencil, others even with a knitting needle; things such as these are less effective than the thumb. In our opinion the little finger is ideal for a thickly charred pipe, and nothing else should be employed, especially as it has the sensitivity essential to the operation of filling, a sensitivity to be found nowhere else.

Special implements of a strange and somewhat fearsome appearance are to be bought intended to fulfill the operations outlined above. They are practical enough but in no way indispensable. A penknife for the curetting and some rounded object with an even surface for packing down the burning tobacco are all the smoker needs. It must not be imagined that a pocket loaded up with a complete smoker's outfit is going to make a good smoke; as well might a fisherman burden himself with every conceivable gadget of the latest invention and wait for the fish to rush to his hook. Things do not work out so, and the wisdom of the ages teaches us that we know no better than our forebears.

To get a quick scrape-out some smokers do not empty their pipe until it is cold. This is a good thing to do so long as the rules on partial cleaning (page 126) are observed and the pipe cleaner is passed through the pipe before the bowl cools off. Porcelain pipes (and in general any pipe made of a metallic material) cool more quickly than briars; it is therefore easier to fill and smoke the same pipe again and again instead of having to alternate it with others in the rack.

Two is the absolute minimum of pipes that a smoker must have. While one cools off the other can be smoked. A true smoker always has several handy, but he cannot carry less than two in his pocket. We ourselves always have four or five about us, which runs flatly contrary to the medical opinion that it is less harmful to stick to the same pipe than to have a collection because, the doctors say, the poisonous deposit that dries up while the pipe is laid aside for a month or two will revive on smoking again and be even more harmful. The only comment worth making on this is that it is of concern only to careless and unhygienic smokers, and that doctors (usually confirmed cigarette smokers themselves) have an unfortunate tendency to call all pipe smokers unhygienic. To determine once and for all these therapeutic controversies— which end in curing no one—Part Four shall be devoted to the subject, and this section will conclude as briefly as may be.

Scraping out a pipe is an operation which finds its complement and its reason solely in the production of more matter to scrape out. It is by curetting and cleaning that the pipe is prepared to make this necessary once again. It is advisable every now and again to take one's pipe to pieces, and here the adherents of the two schools of thought on the question of scraping can settle among themselves what is to be done. Those who have followed our advice will be left in no doubt or trouble. It is not until a pipe has been thoroughly cleaned and dried that a smoker can embark lightheartedly on the less arduous task of making it necessary to clean and dry it once again.

Part Four

THE PIPE AND HEALTH

MEDICAL OPINION is fairly evenly divided on the question of the effects of tobacco on the human system. Some denounce only nicotinism as a sort of intoxication brought about by the abuse of tobacco. Others condemn tobacco outright, and among them many great names such as that of Buffon, Goethe, Heine, Tolstoy, Stendhal are associated, as well as others that have not been dead long enough to become great. But not everything is good for everyone, as the preacher tells us, and everyone does not profit by everything. To us it appears that only excess is to be condemned as in other things, and excess in drinking Vichy water is as much to be reprehended as excess in drinking alcohol.

However, as the pros and contras have never shown up so clearly as in this instance how relative are opinions out of the realm of practice and the individual, it would be a pity to deprive ourselves of the pleasure of confronting them with one another. So let us amuse ourselves for a time, in complete ignorance of the causes but in full acquaintance with the effects.

Nicotine is usually placed by the side of belladonna, between the vascular and the cardiac poisons, so it is none of your common venom. A lethal dose varies from 50 mgs. to 60 mgs. according to the tobacco employed. Chemical research has succeeded in separating from tobacco smoke (apart from its basic components) traces of malate or maleic acid salt, citrate of nicotine, pyridine, collidine, methylamin, prussic acid, ammoniac, and carbon monoxide. All these components "enjoy" a varying degree of toxicity, according to the doctors. They declare that the slow, gentle smoking so beloved of smokers favors the formation of carbon monoxide, to which they attribute most of the troubles caused by smoking. It is that which vitiates the atmosphere surrounding the smoker and poisons him little by little. Yet some scientists assert that the quantity of this poison being so small it can have no influence on the pathogenesis of smoking. We join with them in declaring that were it so, nonsmokers would be equally poisoned if they frequented the places where smoking was taking place, if there was no proper airing. The question of carbon monoxide can therefore be eliminated as it is not found solely in tobacco.

Professor R. says that the smoker of light tobacco is a candidate for cancer* because the tar contained in nicotine is a well-known cause of that disease. Mucous membrane subjected every day to a coating of such tar presents, after six months, very clear lesions. But Dr. P. certifies that the components of nicotine are totally destroyed or decomposed by the combustion of the tobacco. In the smoke produced by tobacco containing one gr. of nicotine not a tenth of that quantity remains, and in the smoke exhaled from the smoker's mouth an even smaller amount, so he absorbs no more than a twenty-fifth part of the nicotine in the unsmoked tobacco. From this analysis, added to the facts presented by Professor R., it appears that the burning of tobacco transforms the nicotine contained in it to such comparatively harmless substances as creosol, phenol or pyridine, which are antiseptics, irritants maybe, but hostile to the growth of bacteria which have need of oxygen to live and multiply.

---

* In particular cancer of the lungs, this being the latest disease in the textbooks of the anti-tobaccoites.

Nicotinism appears under two forms: *chronic*, which manifests itself in such local symptoms as pharyngitis, sialarrhœa or abnormal formation of saliva, and bad breath, or in general symptoms such as dyspepsia, cephalalgia or headache, troubles of the eyesight or of the memory; and *acute,* the symptoms of which are depression, anxiety, pallor, sweating, vertigo, dyspnœa or difficulty of breathing, vomiting, uncontrollable yawning.

In addition to these complaints we find: dental caries, mental ailments, physical and moral depression, nicotinic paralysis, amnesia, paraplegia, muscular ataxia, paralysis of the heart, angina pectoris, embolisms, amaurosis, apoplexy, epilepsy, stomatitis, cirrhosis, hiccoughs, neuralgia of the arms and shoulders, alterations in the senses of hearing and taste, diminution of appetite, and—as we want to leave nothing out—tabacosis or a form of pneumoconiosis which attacks workers in tobacco factories, and softening of the brain. This last can be observed also in nonsmokers and notably such tobaccophobes as Alexandre Dumas *fils.*

In short, everything is to be imputed to tobacco, and for centuries doctors have put to its account all the diseases and maladies they have found themselves unable to cure. That is why we can with a good heart see how they contradict one another. If one listens to Dr. K. dyspepsia results from smoking in the morning on an empty stomach; but Dr. S. advises us to do so in order to avoid constipation—a cigar, says he, has a laxative benevolence on many subjects who "practice it."

A great number of doctors are in accord as to the harm done by tobacco to the respiratory system, but this does not prevent Professor G. from presenting statistics that speak for themselves regarding angina pectoris. Out of 200 cases he found 42 women who did not smoke, 54 men who had never smoked or had ceased from doing so for some years, leaving 104 smokers of all kinds. Statistics collected in other countries and on other ailments are neither more contradictory nor more convincing.

Naturally many oculists attribute certain eye troubles to nicotine, notably amblyopia or dimness of sight; but others put this weakness down solely to the use of alcohol, which seems more reasonable. For it should be noted that, contrary to what happens in the case of alcohol, a strong dose of tobacco smoke causes no definite lesions but only temporary ones.

Professor R., as we have seen, attributes cancer to the tar content of nicotine. Those who share his view say that the case is graver when the subject smokes a short pipe or "nose-warmer." This makes one smile. In America a certain Mrs. Lage Gaston undertook a furious campaign against tobacco which savored more of egocentricity than philanthropy. She, too, was among those who accuse tobacco of being the cause of cancer. This notion became such an *idée fixe* with her that she demanded that smokers should be liable to legal proceedings, all for their own good of course. It was of the irony of things that she herself died of cancer of the mouth. It is as dangerous to speak against tobacco as it is to interfere without having anything to say! Ptyalism, or excessive flow of saliva, is a complaint by no means confined to smokers; it may even be caused by too much zeal in trying to convert smokers, especially when it is muddled up with philanthropy, as in the case of Mrs. Lage Gaston.

To all who are not smokers (for a smoker, like a poet, is born and like him can never be cured of his malady) and find it easy to give to others from the superabundant excess of their own virtue (which is really but an absence of vice) we can suppose arguments as cogent as any they produce, both pro and contra. But this is not a treatise on what may be called Tabacology, and we are not concerned with the defense of tobacco. The trouncing it has received from the high priests of armchair sport, and from the "hearty" theoretical fresh-air fiends, will not disturb the equilibrium of the pipe smoker who never suffers from tobacco intoxication. It is simply to put the facts on record that we report these

maneuvers in the Tobacco War, which in some points resembles
the Opium War.

When coffee was first introduced from the Far East it met with
the same opposition. It was prohibited by the Sherif of Mecca,
forbidden to enter Constantinople, attacked by the medical pro-
fession as soon as it reached Western Europe. It was not until
some Armenians conceived the idea of opening an establishment
to sell coffee in Paris that society fell for the new vice. Snobbery,
fashion and finally the appreciation of the bourgeoisie did the
rest.

Like coffee, tobacco has no longer any need to be defended. It is
no more poisonous than any other intoxicant partaken of by man
—from intellectualism, byway of politics, to rotgut whisky. These
questions of harmfulness or harmlessness must not be taken seri-
ously or one will end by being mentally intoxicated oneself. It is
enough to pick up any medical book to find enumerated a most
amazing list of ailments and maladies, some of them quite fashion-
able; inability properly to assimilate knowledge leads to mental
indigestion. A little knowledge is a dangerous thing. The first dose
of it bowls us over because, being undigested, it makes us sick;
culture is not necessarily knowledge so much as a belief that one
knows a lot—self-imagined knowledge. So the pros and contras
should be debated good-humoredly. "Tobacco makes one shake
with laughter," wrote Neander in his book on the subject. It
should be so with all disputes; what else are they for?

Medicine accepts tobacco as an antiseptic. Careful research has
proved that it checks the development of a number of bacilli, in-
cluding Koch's bacillus. Some doctors advocate its use not only
by means of inhaling but also by chewing, the sanguinary system,
they say, taking 9 mg. of nicotine to the liter, or approximately
1½ pints, of blood. It has been found that those who favor chewing tobacco (*tabacum aptum mundi*) are immune from dental
caries, and that those who take snuff (*tabacum pulveratum*) clear

their nasal cavities while stimulating the sense of smell by exciting the pituitary membrane; though the abuse of the habit may well destroy this sense and cause irritation of the mucous membrane and troubles in the Eustachian tube.

There is no need to indulge in chewing or snuff-taking, as tobacco smoke contains enough nicotine to ensure good asepsis in the mouth. A great number of tobacco experts agree that tobacco containing less than 2 per cent of nicotine is innocuous, in the sense that the elimination of this quantity is effected in the course of absorption. Few tobaccos are sold with a greater nicotine content than 2.5 per cent, and most with less than 2 per cent, so we should be well advised to pay little heed to these objections. Tobacco being aseptic, it will preserve the teeth so long as they are otherwise taken care of, but it is no remedy for neglect.* This aseptic quality is noticeable where certain contagious diseases are concerned, some smokers being rendered immune. During a cholera epidemic in Spain it was verified that the scourge affected very slightly those who smoked heavily. This immunity, also enjoyed by workers in the tobacco factories, goes to prove that tobacco checks or prevents the development of pathogenic germs. At Genoa, in 1889, when the city was in the throes of a severe influenza epidemic, not a single case occurred among the tobacco workers.

Tobacco is also an excellent vermifuge, and it prevents constipation. It is good against scurvy and glossoplegia, or paralysis of the tongue (as Mrs. Lage Gaston might have learned to her advantage) as well as of catarrhal deafness. It may cause headache when taken in excess, but an infusion of it will cure this, as was the case with Marie de' Medici. Nicotine is greatly appreciated as an enema. The famous breaker of wind (or to use a good English word, "farter") who astounded (or deafened) the world in 1890 had no

---

* Nicotine can be employed in the form of soap or toilet cream for the treatment of scabies and certain other skin conditions.

other secret than that he gave himself an enema of tobacco smoke before appearing on the stage. So it is clear that the ingestion of the plant is harmless. At the other end, *i.e.* the head, in normal doses tobacco excites the faculties of the intellect. Recourse is often had to it in cases of apoplexy or lethargy.

So far as longevity is concerned it has been proved by statistics that the greater the smoker the longer he lives. A number of centenarians have been fiends for smoking. Statistics, again, prove that the expectation of life has been longer since the introduction of tobacco and its use by the ordinary man. Taking the example of France: in 1830 the average duration of life was no more than twenty-eight years; in 1953 it is forty-five years, the consumption of tobacco in proportion to the population having trebled in that period. This increase in the average duration of life is most marked among those peoples who beat the record for the consumption of tobacco, such as the Dutch and the Swiss.

It is said that tobacco is a handicap in athletics. We do not believe this. After considerable experience and research we consider that it depends entirely on what one may call the dosage. Primitive man, who led a life of much more physically violent activity than we do—hunting, fishing, fighting, dancing—smoked and, indeed, still smokes more than we do. Unbroken contact with Nature taught him the art of taking things in their proper proportion; this art we have lost, for much of the "nerves" we suffer from—especially in the case of cigarette smokers—comes from a lack of this balance and proportion. It is observable that smoking is heaviest among government and other officials as well as members of the liberal professions. Sporting men in general, being more in contact with real life, know better how to control their appetites. Athletes are usually great smokers, but they abstain before a game. Even while training, Georges Carpentier used to smoke a cigarette after every meal. As to flying men, they are notoriously heavy smokers.

In short, why is there so much agitation about this perfectly innocent plant? Its misdeeds have been studied one after another, but would this have been so had not the ordinary man continued to inhale the smoke of its dried leaf? The fearful smoker's cancer, fluttered like a black flag before the adolescent sufferer from hay fever or a cutaneous eruption—maybe he has ventured to smoke a cigarette without the family doctor's approval—is pure invention. That cancer may come to heavy smokers if they are also syphilitics, was the dictum of a well-known professor. This makes the matter clearer, for in such a case cancer is but one of the numerous complications that victims of syphilis are liable to; tobacco has nothing to do with the origin of the disease; if the malady did not show itself in this form it would do so in some other. A healthy man cannot contract syphilis—he could as easily contract a bad headache.

Amid all these arguments and discussions we should not lose sight of the fact that the pleasure of smoking is not only sensual but intellectual. If some men of art and literature have declaimed against it, others have been good smokers. The numbers of pipe smokers are legion. One recalls Arthur Rimbaud's letter to his friend Ernest Delahaye, "I smoke my pipe by the window and spit on the tiles"; Baudelaire in verse and Mallarmé in prose have celebrated the pipe. J. M. Barrie's *My Lady Nicotine* is a panegyric few have equaled. Tobacco has given us works of art and has been the inspiration of great masters. It has been the solace of men of action from Jean-Bart to General Leclerc, from Sir Walter Raleigh to Sir Winston Churchill.

"A man who smokes," said Fourrier, "is a man who perishes." Such a categorical statement can but make one smile when one sees the effect of smoking on longevity. What about the man who drinks? "Tobacco and alcohol," said Dumas *fils,* "are the most redoubtable foes of the intellect." If that be so, we can but assume that he was a secret smoker, in view of the complete failure of his intellect at the end. Fortunately we have Balzac on our side, when he wrote that tobacco was a cure for "the sickness of civilization."

Opinion being divided, and great names being marshaled on both sides, let us go back to Baudelaire and his *Artificial Paradise* which, though devoted to the cause of opium, shows in some of its immortal pages that smoking is as exciting to the sense of "The Beyond" as it is to the sense of normal smell. Sight seeming to be the key sense of the present age, and smell its poor relative in the family of senses, the practice of pipe smoking will restore this latter, draw it from its chrysalis and regain for it the dignity that our senses have lost since the days of the caveman who, according to Baudelaire, was even able to hear the grass grow.

In lifting the debate to a worthy level, one which few but artists have placed it upon, the pipe will be removed from the smoke of a fruitless discussion beneath the dignity of its nature. Talk about tobacco should be avoided; it can stand on its own merits. The effect of tobacco on the human organism varies with this latter. A deficient system cannot support it; neither can it support strong brandy, or wine taken to excess, while even milk can make one sick if it is forced down. A pipe smoked at the right moment can be as nourishing as a cordial. Rum can do harm, but at the critical moment it may strengthen the system. A vegetarian diet does not make for thinness, and a man with a weak heart will do better to dine off breast of fowl than a dish of cucumber.

Everything can be good and everything bad, according to circumstances. The stomach secretes corrosive juices—for the great benefit of the system. The man who understands himself will keep well. Even a sweet, well-seasoned pipe can, if smoked at the wrong time, produce as disastrous an effect as a virgin pipe. On the other hand, what about the condemned man's last cigarette—his final tenuous link with the pleasures of this world?

We have said that smokers, like poets, are born; this applies especially to pipe smokers. Some men's systems cannot bear a pipe; but to make this an argument against the pipe in general would be absurd.

A pipe is an eternal object. Tobacco always requires a tube of some sort, but in the cigarette it is the tobacco alone that draws; in the pipe the wood container plays its part in the operation of smoking. It is enough to smoke a cigarette made of denicotinized tobacco, and then a pipe of the same, to appreciate the truth of this. Where the pipe is sapid, grateful to the taste, the cigarette is insipid; for the wood container bears to the olfactory nerve the necessary titillation, just as a single grain of pepper gives a flavor to tasteless meat.

It is worth considering how much less susceptible to the harmful effects of nicotinism is a pipe smoker as compared with a smoker of cigarettes. Yet the consumption of cigarettes in Europe has more than doubled since 1920 despite all the increases in price and other restrictions. Which goes to prove that therapeutic questions weigh lightly with ordinary folk. Many writers in the nineteenth century predicted a sad future for the cigarette; they were far from true prophets. The increase of smoking by women has sent the consumption of cigarettes up to astronomical figures. It would appear from incomplete statistics that over the age of forty men increasingly tend to take to a pipe. There is nothing remarkable in this. Between the cigarette and the pipe is a gulf that not even the same brand of tobacco can bridge. The cigarette smoker takes as much pleasure in swallowing or inhaling his smoke as in savoring its aroma; the pipe smoker very rarely inhales. It follows from this that intoxication is much sooner reached by the former, since the smoke passes directly into the blood stream through the pulmonary cells. The rapid burning of a cigarette makes the pleasure of smoking of short duration, consequently one cigarette is lit from the stub of its predecessor and so the chain goes on. Little by little the smoker will begin to experience a distaste that he will attribute to the quality of the tobacco—and he may be not far wrong—or to the state of his mouth; yet come what may he will go on smoking one cigarette after another, getting the less pleasure the faster he smokes. To him smoking is at once a necessity and a luxury; he seems to enjoy the sight of the rings he makes as much as the aroma, it relieves his boredom or calms his nerves. In short, it is a form of intoxication. He is less the master of his cigarette than a pipe smoker of his pipe, attributing to it virtues it cannot—could not—possibly enjoy. He is attached to his tobacco exclusively—how could he be otherwise with a paper container that vanishes with the cigarette!

The man who rolls his cigarettes is less a slave or dupe. He at least contributes something by his skill in rolling; it is within his power to make a good or a bad cigarette. He may make it thin or thick, tight or loose—it is partly his creature, he has scope for his own personality. Mechanically made cigarettes sold in packets have made smoking become nothing but a bad habit instead of a real pleasure. Only those who roll can claim any balanced equilibrium among cigarette smokers.*

During the war years various shortages of tobacco have told heavily on the pipe smokers, many of whom have abandoned the briar for the cigarette—to get intoxication faster and more cheaply. At first they did not realize that tobacco could be taken except through the medium of a pipe, but little by little they learned otherwise. It cost too much to smoke a pipe. At first they never refused a cigarette but after a whiff or two of it they packed the remainder into the pipe. But even as a man can become a confirmed drinker, so they have become confirmed cigarette smokers, and only seldom have they returned by degrees to the pipe. Intoxication has them in its grip, intoxication pure and simple. Only the nostalgia for a pipe and the increasing distaste for confected tobacco will drag such a victim out of the grip of nicotin-

* They must be distinguished from those who use a pocket machine for making their cigarettes.

ism. Yet such smokers realize all the time that there is no comparison between what they have and what they have lost. They long to regain the robustness, the healthiness that was theirs when they smoked a cut. They have lost a certain equilibrium that the pipe gave them, even in times of dearth. We would affectionately advise them to try a small pipe, smoke it new, and not go back to the old pipes that have for so long been lying in a drawer. The delight of seasoning new pipes will bring a man back into the circle of genuine smokers.

It cannot be denied that compared with the pipe smoker the cigarette addict seems a sick man. The pipe smoker, having taken his pleasure at ease with one pipe, will take his time before filling another. One smoke having left him satisfied, he will clean his pipe properly before selecting another. The burning of a medium-sized pipe, that shown on page 49, for example, should last not less than an hour. The smoker should scarcely be able to see that he is smoking; his technique is such that he seems to exhale no smoke. It is laughable to read the legend of Sir Walter Raleigh—as redoubtable a poet as an adventurer—that "his servant seeing his master wreathed in smoke, thought that he had caught fire and threw a pailful of water over him." Raleigh was either a very bad smoker or there was something other than tobacco in his pipe.

The most harmful element in a cigarette is the paper. When the smoker has got through his packet or two in a day he has swallowed a quantity of paper smoke as harmful in itself as half a pound of tobacco, for this paper is made to smolder by the addition of such lethal products as nitrate of calcium and nitrate of magnesium. Why rave about the dangers of nicotine? Nicotine is harmless compared with paper.

How much wiser it is to give oneself over to the pleasures of a cigar, which possesses none of the drawbacks of the cigarette and comes to us free of all artificial matter, in all its candid nudity save for the band that is immediately thrown away. Some assert that the cigar preceded the pipe; the *cohiba* of the South American Indians on page 66 must be its ancestor. This may be so, but a discussion on the subject would take us too far, for the history of the cigar is as closely concerned with that of the pipe as the history of the latter with that of tobacco. Suffice it to say that so far as we are concerned it dates only from Regency days, from a period when the middle class felt sure of itself only when it had a cigar between its teeth. Cigars and smokers were made for one another, both fat and both with gaudy rings. George Sand smoked "like a miner," alternating her cigars with little pipes; others such as Sir Winston Churchill have made the cigar a characteristic feature of their personality; yet despite all this, cigar smoking is on the decline; the cigar has given way before the cigarette and the pipe in all countries. This is an age of nerves, and man has taken to the cigarette as the more satisfying from that aspect.

The constitution of a cigar, in its homogeneity and makeup, has no similarity to that of a pipe. It is composed of:

1. The interior or core, made of bruised and torn leaves placed lengthwise.
2. The first envelope of half-leaves surrounding the core.
3. The cloak or robe of thin strips of leaves wrapped in a spiral round the first two parts.

The cigar thus constituted can certainly produce excellent results—not comparable to a pipe, of course—in keeping with the quality of the tobacco employed, the best of which is from Havana. Being free of any paper deterioration, as in the cigarette, cigars kept in a wooden box can be preserved for fifty years; the smoking of a cigar should take not less than an hour.*

All we have said on the thousand and one fashions of smoking

* We refer to the ordinary cigar, not to the "niños" or to the true cheroot which is so huge in girth that Europeans quail at the sight of it.

invariably leads us back to the pipe. It is irreplaceable, there is nothing to come up to it. It is a part of Nature, the male element in the "fumicological" system. It is the friend of noncompetitive sport, an indispensable feature of any genuine camping outfit. It may be said to strengthen the jaws of those who use it, it gives strength to the gums and the teeth alike. In war it is supreme, for it is more to be trusted than a cigarette; it is adapted to the violent life so dear to all true adventurers. But it reigns also in times of peace where calm and sedate-minded men smoke and plan for the future, men of Jupiter and Saturn, as the astrologers love to call them, men of the open air who never confound reality with the confusion of the day, nor the interior life with some vague Utopia.

If the pipe is no enemy to men who live a violent life, it is a true friend to those who suffer from nerves. It can elucidate complexes, soften rancor, appease excitement, solve problems. It gives the system an equilibrium as material as it is spiritual. "There is something in a pipe that can make a man stable in mind," a modern author says, and in certain cases nothing can give so much confidence in a person of whom we know nothing, though we have to do business with him, as to learn that he is a pipe smoker.

In 1617, while he was exploring the Mississippi, Marquette met an Indian chief who passed his calumet to the traveler with the words, "My son, I give you this that you may know my heart."

Part Five

SOME LAST QUESTIONS

Is a pipe subject to the laws of old age, or does it enjoy eternal youth? Is a very well seasoned pipe better than one that has only just begun to ripen? Does it always progress in excellence without going backward? Is there any evolution beyond the limits of the excellent?

From personal experience we have observed: Evolution from virginity to maturity; then a stationary condition.

No doubt this will be contested by many well-intentioned smokers, and will lead to regrettable carelessness in some beginners. But it must always be remembered that we are seasoners of the Third School (page 139) and naturally lean to the virgin pipe rather than the heavily charred pipe, especially if it be a briar. For us, the best thing is the char proper, and we belong to this Third School solely because it furthers the production of this to the maximum. As we have said earlier, circumstances play a great part in the circumscribed region round the bowl of a pipe, circumstances depending on the organic, on the atmospheric, and we were going to say on the telluric state of the subject on the one hand, and on the other the ambience, where it dies, of the orbit of which the pipe is the center. This cannot be enclosed within determined limits.

Smokers who keep in reserve five or six pipes in a virgin state sometimes like to return to the old-stagers for a smoke. Why is this? It is because a pipe is never dead. If it gets dull, loses its charm, ceases to draw properly, it is better to let it sleep, to forget it, leave it, and some fine day come on it again all covered with dust but full of fragrance and overflowing with memories. Some pipes left as dead for five years have begun a new existence on being lit once again.

Except in a case of hopeless fouling, what a very great mistake it would be to destroy a pipe as being finished and done for. It is very rare that the bowl of a pipe chars right through to the outside. But even then it is better to give it to a friend than to destroy it; it may be just his pipe! Maybe he is the one person in the world who can recall it to life. It is with a pipe as with a woman: she may mean nothing to you but all the world to some other man. A pipe has its individual taste as well as the taste we help it to acquire; it is not always the pipe that changes, it may well be the smoker. What is this in front of us, decayed, shaped outlandishly, shabby, what is it but the pipe stowed away in the attic of some smoker dead these fifty years, whose name is cursed by his descendants. Yet on examining the seasoning of this pipe we can learn that its late possessor was a remarkable man, and declare loudly that we should be proud to claim him as our ancestor.

Let us rejuvenate the old pipes with alcohol. They will come again into their own with all the experiences and reminiscences of a long journey. No words could ever describe the beauties of their emanations; there will be an unexpected cachet in it, waiting for us to savor it. Pipes can be very interesting, as Sherlock Holmes observed. Nothing, he said, had more individuality than a pipe, except maybe a watch or a bootlace.

You must have come across cigarette smokers who, with wistful glances at your pipe remarked, "Ah yes, I smoked one once upon a time," in much the same sad way as one says, "Once I was young." How one would like to tell them that it is "up to them" to be young again, to renew that long-lost pleasure. On closer questioning you will find the reasons for their having given up a pipe most obscure, though never once have I heard of health being given as one of them.

Out of a hundred smokers about eighty have tried a pipe at some time or another; of these fifty meant to persevere; of this fifty half have given up the attempt after an honest trial. Yet among those failures there were some individuals really born to smoke a pipe. Their defeat proves nothing; it certainly cannot be imputed to the pipe, which ever retains its own worth, a worth that only he who smokes it can appreciate. The man who gives up a pipe because he cannot fill it properly, or light it, or has made a bad choice in the first place, is denying himself the source of a daily and voluptuous pleasure; he sells himself to the cigarette and the evils of nicotinism.

It is to the cigarette smoker in particular that we address the following remarks. Maybe he has imagined that a pipe could be smoked as simply as a cigarette, and its smoke swallowed; and he may be disappointed to find that it is not so. Yet there will be moments when he feels the lack of something within him, a sense of not being satisfied, an indefinable longing. Do not let him neglect these yearnings. The crisis of life is often met in the passing moment, just as the fruit when it is ripe suddenly falls from the tree and bursts upon the ground. Let him not miss the moment nor neglect the inspiration; let him take to himself a pipe and fill it. Some other man, maybe, on reading this book may desire to make the attempt at smoking a pipe on his own account; if so, let him go to a reliable shop and select a good pipe. He will find that our words and advice are not mere sentences thrown to the wind if we have awakened in him a nostalgia that he is able to satisfy. The day will soon come when he will abandon his cigarette and smoke his pipe, enjoying it and not intoxicating himself.

Is there any special moment during the day when smoking is better than at other times? Some say it is after a meal, especially after dinner or supper. Far be it from us to contradict them, but it depends on one's way of life rather than on any advice we can give. Besides, what sort of dinner is meant? An overfed millionaire's?

Athletes training for long-distance walking and faced with a day of strenuous physical effort frequently fill themselves with nicotine before starting. To stand this they must be absolutely fit, which means that the blood circulates freely throughout their bodies, and that they can enjoy a pipe far more than the son of the family whose idea of life is confined to the pavement of his native town—even if it be the capital. Such a lad is just the type for a cigarette, unless Nature has endowed him with sense and a more than common olfactory sensitivity.

A pipe on an empty stomach can be as satisfying as one lit during the alimentary stasis that precedes digestion. There is the "first pipe of the day" just as there is the "first cigarette"; each is unique according to how one looks at it. As a digestive or an aperitif, as a solace by day or night, summer or winter, familiar as an old friend, the pipe retains all the charm of the unforeseen, the unexpected. The aroma it emits is unique, even to the senses of those who do not smoke, as can be demonstrated by thrusting a pipe in the plenitude of its effluence under the nose of such a one. Its bouquet invariably causes surprise, it sometimes makes a convert, it always amazes. In direct contact with this emanation, the critical sense has no chance to react, it is reduced to impotence. It is, alas, a sign of the moral state of our times that this momentary conversion is lasting only among those few rare souls who care nothing for weariness and discouragement, but love to swim against the current.

Courage is needed to live at all; yet greater courage is required to enjoy life.

We have said that the pipe is eternal. Its outward shape may change, may evolve, may possibly modernize, but the principle of bowl-mouthpiece remains forever immutable.

The briar pipe industry has its birthplace and home at Saint-Claude, but although an industry, it does not produce "standard" articles. The craftsman knows and cares nothing as to how the pipe he makes is to be presented for sale. He cuts it from the block even as a statue is liberated from the marble by the hand of the sculptor. Each pipe has its own individuality. Every briar root has once been alive, has survived the perils of growth, has thriven in its particular patch of soil, and developed its own hydrography.* The same series of roots may contain powerful and individual personalities, quite independent of the design of the manufacturer. No two pipes are exactly alike; there are no analogies amongst them, as can be found in human faces or characters. Identical twins are rare, even then it is rare that they look exactly alike, rarer still that their personalities are indistinguishable, most rare of all is any similarity in their destinies. So it is with pipes cut from the same stock. Each is unique in itself. The pipe emerges from nonexistence; it is worked upon, it is titivated—but it is we who put the finishing touch to it, who crown the achievement by smoking it.

But while virgin, the pipe remains a Sleeping Beauty. It is not until the first whiff of smoke has risen from the bowl that its true life begins. So let us awaken it—and when awake may it prove the true Pipe of Peace, reminding us that we are all brothers.

---

* In America, at the time of its discovery, the place where clay was dug to make the calumets was declared a consecrated site, so that pipes could continue to be made in times of war.

CONCLUSION

Surrounding a man in every aspect of his life there are two kinds of objects—the Useful and the Useless—or what we think useless. Ask that man you pass in the street which he would rather have, a fountain pen or a pipe, and he will very rightly choose the former. Nevertheless, we still enjoy the useless. In most gardens you will find more trees than are actually needed to furnish shade, nor are they grown for firewood, nor, for the matter of that, are the gardens themselves solely for the cultivation of vegetables. In the same way, you will see people fond of animals, and not just domestic animals or those required for food. We cultivate flowers, hang pictures on walls, carry nameless and numberless things in our pockets that can be of no more use than the marbles of our childhood—yet nothing of all these is so much as expected to prove Useful.

These Useless things stay with us forever, they are eternal. No need to seek some justification for their existence, to enquire whether they are beloved by us or mere matters of indifference, to cast a doubt upon them in any way—they are there. Wanted or not, they are there. Maybe they are in some sort the totems of our tribe.

Man certainly makes free with the living things the earth sets before him. He kills tigers, puts them in cages, gives them scientific names. The day will come before long when the dog will disappear from our streets and suffer the same eclipse as the horse, which in its turn supplanted the reindeer. Man is never content until he has taken the beautiful, free creatures of the earth, the living grandeur of Creation, stuffed them to put in museums, and robbed them of all nobility. A day will come when he will regret having exterminated the tiger, done away with the dog, lost the horse; and then he will attempt to recreate them by scientific means.

What is considered useful is given first place. Money is useful, but bank notes are none the less the greatest germ carriers on this planet, and the man who blames his neighbor for sucking at a pipe will suck his own thumb as he counts his notes.

When Nature feigns death she stands more chance of surviving, since none perceives her. She makes no challenge to the pride of man, she clings to this challenge in the secrecy of her own heart. One would think less of drowning a dog than of throwing a pipe in the dustbin—but then a dead dog cannot be awakened, but there will always be found men everywhere who will awaken a pipe.

About the Author

Born in Montauban in southern France in 1912, Georges Herment studied at the universities of Toulouse and Paris. His great enthusiasm was jazz, and after taking part in several programs of the Hot Club of France he became a professional musician, a career which was interrupted by the outbreak of the war in 1939.

Herment served on the Eastern front and then on the Belgian frontier, where, after thirty-five days of combat, he was taken prisoner and sent to Pomerania. He escaped in June of 1941, crossed all of Germany and was recaptured at the Italian frontier. Shipped back to the Baltic, he again escaped in October of the same year, made his way across Belgium and crossed the demarcation line between Occupied France and Free France in November 1941.

Jazz was forbidden in France at that time, so Herment did a little of everything, from agricultural labor to bike-taxi driving. When the Germans invaded all of France, his case, as that of an escaped prisoner, fell under the jurisdiction of the Vichy government. Unable to cross the Spanish border, he hid on a farm along with the Spanish resistance chief, and there he wrote a book, Evade d'Allemagne, about his escapes. He hid the manuscript until Liberation, and the book was published in 1945. Previously, his only other literary work had been a volume of poetry, Déluges, which won the Brussels poetry prize in 1937.

In 1950 Herment married an Englishwoman and settled in the valley of Aveyron. The Pipe was written there, and has been followed by a novel which was published recently in France.

Since the latter part of 1954, Herment has been living in England on "The Water Gypsy," A. P. Herbert's houseboat.

NOTES

NOTES

NOTES

NOTES

NOTES

NOTES

NOTES

NOTES

NOTES

NOTES